Business as a Holy Calling?

A workbook for Christians
in business and their pastors

Tim A Dearborn

Tim A Dearborn

Special Edition
Mennonite Economic Development Associates

I was blessed to learn that Tim wrote this book and even more
so as I read it. *Business as a Holy Calling?* embodies the mission
of MEDA's members. It's as if he was writing with MEDA's
constituency in mind. *Business as a Holy Calling?* can be used for
many applications: as inspiration for pastors as they strive to
minister to entrepreneurs and business leaders in their
congregations; as a great resource for MEDA's Network Hubs
to help guide discussions, or as the basis for a series of
meetings; or as a helpful guide for individuals to use as they
reflect on their experiences and journey of faith and work.

--Michael White, Chief Strategic Engagement Officer, MEDA

ISBN-13:978-1505570984
ISBN-10:1505570980

Printed in the United States of America

Scripture quotations are from the New Revised Standard Version of the Bible, copyright © 1989 by the Division of Christian Education of the National Council of Churches of Christ in the USA. All rights reserved. Used by permission.

3rd Edition, April 2016

Cover photos: Luke Rattan; cover design courtesy of Dale Kegley and BeckyJo Bourgeois: Seattle Pacific University

TABLE OF CONTENTS

INTRODUCTION

CENTRAL QUESTION: In what ways have you tended only to appreciate business instrumentally—as a means to other ends? What is your reaction to the notion that business has an intrinsic role in the purposes of God?

A GLARING OMISSION AND A NEW REFORMATION

One Sunday, our church was commissioning its youth group to go to Tijuana to build houses. Professional carpenters and an owner of a construction company accompanied them, and were commissioned with them. It occurred to me, "Why were we commissioning them for this volunteer ministry, but we've never thought of commissioning members who were in the construction business for their work building and remodeling homes and offices in Seattle?" Was the same work they did in their daily business now "mission" because it was an "official" church program?

As a pastor, I realized that I was more interested in people's volunteer time, and charitable giving than in their daily work. I focused on people's personal lives, family life, and spirituality—and on recruiting them to volunteer in church sponsored ministries, and on the few who became "full-time" church-funded ministers, missionaries, and urban workers.

I called people either to change what they were currently doing or to add more on top of their already full lives. Give more, do more, care more, serve more were my constant themes.[1] Become full-time Christian workers. Yet in so doing I inadvertently discredited most of the members of my church by implying they were less committed than those in "full-time" Christian ministry. Who were they serving 40 to 60 hours a week in their jobs and family life—their ambitions? Their greed? Their ego? Their boss? I was interested in their volunteer time, not their business life. My interest in their work life stopped with their charitable contributions. The financial fruit of their work interested me more than how they made that fruit.

Since then, for the past 30 years, it has been a great delight to learn from and support people, especially those in business, to discover God's purposes for their work—and particularly for business. The ideas explored in this book have been developed through teaching business school and seminary courses, workshops with business persons, a small group of Christian CEOs with whom I met for a year, and with the leaders of World Vision International's microfinance organization. Focus groups and "beta version" seminars in a dozen churches have further tested and refined the materials. As a "work in progress," I welcome readers' comments and suggestions for how this resource can be improved. Contact information is given at the end of the book.

One evening my wife and I hosted a Buddhist priest from Tokyo who was studying English in Seattle. His eyes lit up as he described his beautiful temple complex outside the Narita airport: ponds, gardens, pagodas, and millions of pilgrims each year. It sounded like a stunning context. Knowing that I was a pastor, he asked if he could see my church. Realizing that my church buildings weren't nearly as impressive as his temple, I said, "That's not very easy to do." I continued, "If you want to see my church, we need to get into

---

[1] For further reflections on this and the transformation in my understanding of mission, see Tim Dearborn, *Beyond Duty: A Passion for Christ, a Heart for Mission* (Dynamis Resources, 2013).

the car and drive to nearly every office building, every school, hospital, and factory, and most of the neighborhoods in our entire region. Your temple sounds like a beautiful place. I'd love to visit it. Our church gathers in a few buildings for a few hours a week, but that's not where the church is. To see it we need to see where they live and work. It is throughout our city and even our world."

A new reformation

Churches are called to equip and support members for their ministry in daily life, not primarily focus on recruiting and drawing members to come to and serve in church programs. The Protestant Reformation emphasized the priesthood of all believers and the sanctity of all work. No one vocation is more pleasing to God than another so long as it doesn't interfere with our life as Christians. All Christians are called to serve God with all their heart, soul, mind, and strength—in whatever work they do. Martin Luther wrote that, "We should accustom ourselves to think of our position and work as sacred and well-pleasing to God."[2] However, the ministry of all believers is often understood today as "lay ministry," the invitation to lay persons to do volunteer church work.

Churches around the world are no longer seeing themselves as the center of ministry. Rather, churches are serving as resources for ministry.

Today we are recovering an understanding that all good work matters to God. We are in the midst of a substantive reshaping of the church's perception of its approach and role in Christians' lives. Rather than limiting its focus to people's personal, spiritual, family, and volunteer life—churches are recognizing their role in equipping and supporting people for their work in the world. Only there can all the people of God fulfill our calling to be ambassadors of God's kingdom as it comes to bear on every aspect of life—business,

---

[2] Martin Luther, "To the Christian Nobility of the German Nation…"
Luther's Works, 44 (Fortress, 1966), 127-130.

government, education, science, medicine, the arts and media, and social service.

There have been dozens of excellent resources written in the past years on a theology of work. It's easy to understand the "Christian" significance of many kinds of work—especially family life, social service, education, and health care. After all, Jesus was involved in all of that. But business—the production and marketing of goods and services for a profit—how does that participate in the coming of the kingdom? If we're supposed to give to the one who asks of us, turn the other cheek, seek the lowest and last place—how can we possibly do business in a Christian way when we've got to make the sale, achieve the targets, get there before our competitors, and demonstrate our skill and expertise to our boss and customers?

CENTRAL CONVICTIONS

Commonly, answers to these questions are found in discussion of ethics—how do we do work in ways that are consistent with God's will and with the values of the kingdom? That is obviously critically important. However, beneath the questions of ethics lie the questions of ends. The purposes of our work and business are integral to its value. We can work hard to abide by a strong code of ethics and conduct in an enterprise that isn't worth doing.

Think for example of the code of conduct among gang members. Loyalty, respect, and obedience are inviolable norms within a gang. Fidelity to this code of conduct is rewarded, and violations are promptly punished.

Throughout this study, we will explore what can make business holy. Our journey will be shaped by several core convictions:

1. **God's purposes for business include far more than profit.**
   Creating employment, generating income, and ensuring profit

are very valuable and vital purposes of business. However, God's purposes go way beyond that.

2. **Business can be, but isn't necessarily, a holy calling.** Business isn't full-time Christian service simply because it's being done by people who are Christian. The "question mark" at the end of the title for this book is placed there intentionally. What has to happen in order for business to be a holy calling?

3. **Most Christians are unclear on the intrinsic purposes of business.** We tend to focus on the *"instrumental"* purposes of business—a means to other ends such as employment, income, Christian witness, and the provision of goods and services. However, it's harder to describe the *"intrinsic"* purposes of business—a good end in and of itself. Business can be embraced as holy when we know how particular products and services fulfill God's purposes for creation and human life.

4. **We need to focus on business purposes, not just business processes.** Rather than exploring business ethics (how we do business in ways that serve God?), this book focuses one step back on business purposes (why we do business as service to God?)

INTENDED OUTCOMES

The goal of this study is that participants come to see how their work currently does—or potentially could—align with God's purposes and be valued as a form of full-time Christian service.

1. **Meaningful conversations** will occur between Christians in business with one another, and with their pastor that can lead to greater support, and deeper alignment between their work and the work of God. Issues pertaining to the integration of our business life with our life of faith aren't often part of church conversations. Therefore, simply creating the opportunity for

our church community engaging together in the on-going pursuit of God's purposes for our life at work in a significant step forward.

2. **Clearer understanding by church leaders** will emerge for how to care for and support their members who are in business.

3. **Deeper awareness by businesspersons** will be gained for how to integrate their business practices with their faith.

4. **The relationships of pastors and Christians in business** with each other and with God will be nourished, and a deeper passion for their participation in God's purposes for business will grow.

5. **Freedom to disagree and dialogue** with others will grow for it is assumed that readers won't agree with all that is said. Everyone approaches these issues with different convictions, and varying amounts of experience and reflection on the topic. This workbook serves as a study guide to facilitate a meeting place for what many Christians in business suggest are long overdue conversations between pastors and businesspersons about God's purposes for business. It creates an opportunity for pastors and persons in business to discuss hard issues and to support and equip one another for service in God's kingdom.

For whom this is written

This book serves as a basis for small group discussions among businesspersons and their pastors. It creates an opportunity for pastors, church leaders, seminary students, and members of their parishes who are engaged in business to have deep, realistic, and candid conversations about the vocation of business.

It is written for people far down the road on their career, as well as those just beginning; for people in transition, and for people who are overwhelmed with their current responsibilities. If you're interested in diving deeper or being more aware of sources for these ideas, explore the footnotes and recommended readings. For those who are pressed for time—you can skip over the extra resources without missing the thrust of the ideas.

It also is written for people at any and all levels in an organization. We will see that everyone has influence, not just those who are "at the top"—the bosses, senior directors and boards. Everyone feels some restraint and limitations—but no one is exempt from the work of aligning their business more closely to the purposes of God.

How to use this workbook

It is designed as a small group or class discussion guide, to enable pastors and businesspersons to explore together God's purposes for business. It is ideal if participants can spend about 1 to 1 ½ hours reading and reflecting before each section. Reflection and discussion questions are provided to aid in personal application and group interaction.

Each section includes an opportunity to "audit" your current organization, and strategize how to bring your own work into closer alignment with the purposes of God. Very few specific suggestions for applying the insights being discussed are provided in the text. This is for two reasons: 1) not to be prescriptive since every person and business context varies; and more importantly, 2) because of the conviction that the Holy Spirit can inspire dynamic creativity within a group as you seek together the implications and applications for your work. Participants are encouraged to bring examples from their own experience. For links to videos and other resources for use with this book, see www.spu.edu/holycalling. See also Seattle Pacific University's extensive collection of resources on business and faith at http://spu.libguides.com/workandfaith.

Typically, groups find an hour and a half meeting is optimal to afford time for discussion and prayer. Another format that I've found to be helpful is to rotate the meeting between each other's workplace. This obviously requires more than an hour and half time commitment. However, seeing where people work, meeting some of their co-workers, having them present an issue they are facing at work as a case study for discussion, and then praying specifically for that individual and their business opens up rich and profound interaction.

CATALYZING ORGANIZATIONAL CHANGE

The following pages may well be the most important ones in this entire study. They outline strategies for catalyzing creative change within our business (or church). It's easy to feel like our influence is limited because of our particular role, and thus assert that there's nothing we can do to bring change. On the other hand, some of us, especially when we are first starting out in a career or job, approach our organization with zealous ideals.

Everyone feels limited in his or her capacity to influence change. A common response when we recognize the discrepancy between the purposes our business serves--and God's greater purposes—is to admit that each of our sphere of influence is limited. For most of us, regardless of our position, others seem to have more influence and control over our work environment than we do—our boss, the CEO, the board, the investors, even the customers. This is frustrating. Our own work and our satisfaction are directly impacted by the culture of the organization as well as how others within it do their jobs.

As a result, our attention is quickly diverted away from the larger, macro-level issues, to the more manageable, issues of personal ethics and relationships. Obviously, our own ethical behavior and loving relationships are integral to God's purposes for our lives.

We may feel that other people impede our ability to do our work well. This is intensified when we have a far-reaching vision about

God's purposes for business and we work part way down an organizational hierarchy. Our influence seems minimal and the discrepancy between what we think is God's will and what we (and our organization) are currently doing may be discouraging. Sometimes our influence is limited because we pursue what could be called "dead-end" strategies. On the other hand, our influence can extend well-beyond our particular responsibilities when we pursue strategies that are life-giving.

> We each have more capacity to exert change on our work environment than we assume.

Dispense with Dead-end Strategies

First, it's important to dispense with unsuccessful strategies to leverage change. These include:

- **Advice-giving**: providing unsolicited recommendations for how others should be doing their jobs

- **Criticizing**: pointing out the flaws in others' ways of working, or in the organizational culture

- **Moralizing**: using every opportunity to sprinkle conversations with words like "must," "should," "ought to"

- **Being a "Know-it-all"**: acting as if I know how to do others' jobs better than they do.

These strategies diminish our influence, our satisfaction, and others' comfort with us. Rather than changing the organization, such a person usually ends by changing organizations.

Adopt Life-giving Strategies

There's a much more fruitful way to catalyze change. Our authority at work extends far beyond our sphere of responsibility. It includes multiple dimensions:

Interests: things that I enjoy doing and find personally fulfilling.

Responsibilities: things that I must do, for they are part of my job description and role.

Concerns: things that I find important to address in order for our organization to be more aligned with what's right, and for me to fulfill my responsibilities more effectively.

Relationships: people who share my responsibilities, have others of their own, and may or may not share my interests and concerns.

Influence: credibility and respect that can permit me to have an impact both within and beyond my area of responsibilities.

Let's develop this in greater detail.

1. Work Where Responsibilities, Interests, and Concerns Meet

- When my responsibilities don't interest me, I'm likely to be bored.

- When I am not concerned with my responsibilities, I'm likely to be ineffective.

- When I try to work outside my responsibilities, I'm trying to do someone else's job and therefore am likely to be seen as a threat or meddler. I may come across as an irritant, insubordinate, not a 'team player,' and probably arrogant.

2. Expand Authority by Increasing Influence

There are several ways to increase our influence. One is to enlarge our responsibility by taking on a bigger job. However, that may not be possible—either because there isn't a job available, I may not be viewed as qualified, and/or increasing my workload may not be consistent with my other priorities in life.

There are other ways to increase influence that are accessible to everyone regardless of one's position in the organization.

- **Fulfill my responsibilities:** My first job is to do my job. I will have no credibility as a catalyst for change if I don't do my work well.

- **Show respect:** If I don't respect my co-workers or organization, it's unlikely I'll be an effective catalyst for change. My suggestions will be perceived as criticisms and rejections, and people are likely to react with irritation or defensiveness.

- **Model the values and change I envision.** Implement the ways of working that I see as worthwhile and consistent with God's will and ways within my area of responsibility. Words of exhortation don't carry much weight. Lived truth does. In those areas I can control, demonstrate the value of doing things differently.

- **Build relationships** with people whose responsibilities extend to concerns that are important to me. I can expand my sphere of influence by building relationships of trust and respect with others. I could do this in a manipulative way—befriending others and showing concern for their interests and well-being to gain my desired ends. That doesn't seem consistent with God's ways. Far better is to build relationships of genuine interest through initiating conversations with people to learn:
  - What do they like about their job?
  - How does it fit with their personal interests and sense of calling in life?
  - Are there ways you could do your job that would help them with theirs'?
  - What do they think about the particular concern that is troubling you? Do they see any ways you could collaborate to help address it? Do they have any advice for you?

11

- **Pray.** God is not limited to our activity. Nor is God limited to our particular sphere of influence. We have authority in Christ that extends far beyond our particular responsibilities and job descriptions. We are ambassadors of Christ's kingdom. Christ holds all authority in heaven and earth—authority over our business, over the people with whom we work, and over the problems and the challenges we face. Our role in catalyzing change is determined more by our position in Christ than our position in the business. Through prayerful participation in what God is doing in our organization, our sphere of influence is likely to grow.

We will never be effective catalysts for change outside our sphere of influence.

Our campaigning for change where we have no credibility does not create our authority in an organization. Rather, our authority is established by effectively fulfilling our responsibilities: doing good work, modeling the change we value, and by building good relationships.

**Sphere of Authority =
Fulfilled Responsibilities
+ Earned Respect
+ Modeled Change
+ Caring Relationships**

In each of the subsequent sections, you will be given opportunities to envision strategies for catalyzing change in specific areas within your sphere of authority as it relates to the topic of that section. Regardless of our level of responsibility in an organization, there are specific ways God can lead and empower us to align our work and life more closely to the purposes of God. Some of the implications may relate directly to our work life. Others, to our life as citizens, consumers, and neighbors. Doing the work to seek specific guidance—and to discuss this with others in your church community—will lead to a clear sense of aligning our lives to God's purposes, and to living with greater joy and freedom.

In preparation, begin by mapping your work life in each of these spheres.

Pray through your current situation, in regard to your interests, responsibilities. What are ways you model what you value? What are areas of work-related concerns that you have which are outside your responsibilities? What are some key relationships you have within your workplace with people who have responsibilities for those areas that concern you?

Spheres of Authority	Current Situation at Work
Interests: What are the things that interest me about my work? If I don't find my work interesting, are there things I could do to make it more so?	
Sphere of responsibility: To what extent does my role coincide with my interests?	
Ways to model the change I value: What can I do within my area of responsibilities to enable my business to align more closely with what I believe to be God's purposes?	
Concerns outside my responsibility: What are issues in my business that concern me but are outside my responsibilities?	

People: Who are people who have responsibilities in those areas, and what can I do to build key relationships to encourage and support others in their spheres of responsibility?	
Prayer: God's engagement with people extends far beyond our own. For what can I pray?	

1. BUSINESS CAN BE A HOLY CALLING

CENTRAL QUESTIONS: What are the dominant emotions you feel about work (besides stress)? What is your response to the idea that business can be as much a place for full-time Christian service as working in a church?

Business can contribute to God's purposes to enable human flourishing and the thriving of creation.

DEFINITIONS OF KEY TERMS

As we begin, it will be helpful to clarify how a few common terms are used in this study:

Christian service: *the work that every follower of Christ does, whether employed by the church, or by a business, or as a volunteer, student, parent, or retired person.*

Kingdom of God: *the reign of God on earth as it is in heaven.*

Heaven: *the Presence of God where God's will and ways are fully realized. Though Heaven in Scripture isn't confined to or the same as earth, the kingdom of God and the kingdom of Heaven are used in the gospels interchangeably.*

Business: *the creation and sale of goods and services. This study focuses particularly on business and not just work in general. Though the ideas explored may be applicable to churches and non-profit organizations, special attention is placed here on for-profit business. Through this study, we will address any suspicion some people might have about the legitimacy of profit-making enterprises.*

Businessperson: *Some people may not necessarily see themselves as a businessperson (such as administrative assistants, clerks, accountants, software developers, bankers, construction laborers, custodians, etc.) However, if they are working in an organization that depends on people purchasing their goods and services to exist (rather than depending on charitable contributions), for the purpose of this study they are engaged in business.*

Economic System: *The way a society organizes the production and exchange of goods and services, and the allocation of resources.*

Capitalism: *An economic system in which investment in and ownership of the means of production, distribution, and wealth exchange are made chiefly by individuals and businesses, rather than cooperatively or by the state.*

Calling (or vocation): *Traditionally this word has been confined to people who believed that God's will was for them to engage in a "religious" occupation—a vocation working within the church. In this study we are asserting something different: all followers of Christ are called, gifted, and guided to participate in specific ways in God's purposes as their particular form of Christian service.*

Holy: *This describes something's relation to the "sacred" and means "pertaining or belonging to God."*

Hearing God's Call Into Ministry

Has it ever struck you as strange about the questions "When did you decide to go into the ministry?" or "How did God call you into full-time Christian service?" The reference is usually in regard to someone who is a pastor, church-worker, or missionary. Are only some people serving God full-time? If so, whom are we serving the rest of our time—our ambitions?

Full-time Christian service isn't the special vocation (calling) of those who are paid by the church to do their work. All followers of Christ are in full-time ministry.

16

Our boss? Our own desires? Our finances? Are our daily lives, and especially the manufacturing and marketing of goods and services for money—dominated by other deities? Aren't all God's people called to serve God with our whole hearts all the time?

For Reflection and Discussion
What's your reaction to the assertion that all Christians are engaged in full-time Christian ministry?

1. A Survey of Attitudes Toward Business as Ministry

Twenty years ago I interviewed over 100 Christian leaders who were well-respected in their professional lives as attorneys, property developers, marketers, CEOs of small businesses, bankers, and other diverse professions. I simply asked around, "Who are the most respected Christian _____ (fill-in the blank) in our community?" I kept a running list of recommended people, and invited them out for coffee, or to join focus groups, so we could talk about their ministry as a Christian attorney, banker, business owner, manager, accountant, software developer, entrepreneur, realtor, etc.

Most of the people with whom I talked were surprised to have their work described as a ministry but no one declined the invitation to talk. I had a series of fascinating conversations in which I asked several questions:

- In what ways, if any, do you see your work as a form of Christian service?
- In what ways, if any, do you receive guidance and support from your church and pastor for the challenges you face at work?
- To what extent does your church value and validate your work-life as a ministry?
- What are the dominant emotions (other than stress) that you feel when you're going to work?
- How do you receive support and guidance as you seek to live out your faith in business?

Here's a summary of what these businesspersons indicated about their work, and their church's support of them in it:

- Few saw their work in business as ministry.

- Few indicated receiving regular and significant guidance from their church for the "nuts and bolts" of their work life. They received guidance about relationships and ethics, but not the daily challenges they faced in business.

- Few had heard business affirmed as a form of full-time Christian service. The notion that it was a "sacred" calling seemed absurd to many.

- Few had a clear notion of how the very nature of their business contributed to God's kingdom. The exceptions were people in health care, education, and social service—since Jesus was involved in those areas.

- Full-time Christian ministry, service of God that really mattered to God, was focused on preachers, pastors, and missionaries. Others provide support so that the religious professionals can do the "real" work of ministry.

- The Reformation's great affirmation of the "priesthood of all believers" and the value of all work were reshaped in their understanding to mean that all Christians, if they are really committed to God, will volunteer in church-based ministries.

- It was difficult for them to imagine business, the manufacturing and marketing of goods and services, as valued as a form of full-time ministry.

These conversations were troubling and grievous. Sure work is hard, and work in business especially so. That's all the more reason for our churches to focus attention on equipping people for the challenges of our daily work. We live in a world that is ravaged by what Christian theology calls "the Fall"—rebellion, self-absorption, and conflict. Studs Terkel begins his famous book, *Working*, with the statement: "This book, being about work, is, by its very nature, about violence—to the spirit as well as to the body."[3] Lest you think this is too severe, it's staggering to note that in a 2013 Gallup survey, 70% of employed Americans indicated they felt disengaged at work, or even hated their jobs.[4]

70% of employed Americans feel disengaged at or even hate their jobs.

Surely that is not God's will for humankind. Yes, following "the Fall," Genesis tells us that we will earn our living by the *"sweat of our brow."* There are *"thorns and thistles"* in the land (Gen 3). Work is hard, but need it do violence to the spirit as well as the body? What does it mean for us not to live *"weary and heavy laden"* lives, and instead to be yoked to Christ, bearing his *"easy and light"* burden (Matt 11:28-30)?

I believe that God's will is for all people to be able to end the day saying, like God did, at the moment of creation, "What I did today was good." And also, "I am grateful for what I was able to do today in service in your kingdom." To the extent that Terkel's statement about the violence of work, and the Gallup poll's summary of people's "hatred" for their jobs are accurate, even in America with all our economic and material privileges, most people would find the invitation to feel gratitude about their work an impossible dream.

For Reflection and Discussion
When was a time you came home from work content and grateful for the privilege of what you were able to do that day?

---

[3] Studs Terkel, *Working*, (The New Press, 1974), 1.
[4] "State of the American Workplace," Gallup, Inc. (June, 2013).
   http://www.gallup.com/services/178514/state-american-workplace.aspx.

2. In Search of the Intrinsic Significance of Business

Since work is indeed hard, and the pressures of business are particularly intense, we would hope that what people do to and for one another during our life at work would be a primary concern of the church. Unfortunately, rather than valuing business as an important way Christians participate in the purposes of God, the Christian businesspersons I interviewed felt their churches valued business as a necessary way to earn an income, and money for the church. Particularly successful businesspersons were valued for ways they could bring credibility to the church. Their service on church committees or on non-profit boards, their volunteer service, their charitable giving, and maybe what they did upon retirement was understood and valued by their church more than the enterprise that dominated 40 to 60 hours of their week. What they heard from their churches pertained more to work in general than to business in particular.

Business is valued instrumentally as a way to:

- **Earn money and create jobs:** We all need money to survive, to care for ourselves, and to care for others.
- **Give money to support the church:** Churches and charities need people to earn money so they can give money. We remember John Wesley's famous adage, "Earn all you can. Save all you can. Give all you can."[5]
- **Enhance respect for the Gospel:** We value businesspersons' success as an opportunity to bring credibility to the church because of the status and success of their position as a Christian who was a CEO, successful real estate developer, or player on the local professional sports team.

---

[5] John Wesley, *The Use of Money*. Sermon 50. http://wesley.nnu.edu/john-wesley/the-sermons-of-john-wesley-1872-edition/sermon-50-the-use-of-money

- **Do evangelism:** Some received admonitions to use their place of work for witness—hosting Bible studies in their office or at lunch, inviting co-workers to church, and getting in a good word for Jesus in the midst of conversations. (Most admitted feeling inadequate or uncomfortable with this).

These are all good things—but they don't speak directly to the intrinsic purpose of business itself. In my small survey of businesspersons, most were surprised by the idea that:

A theology or spiritual understanding of manufacturing airplanes, selling cars, marketing products, designing electrical systems, selling plumbing parts, and litigating lawsuits was unimaginable and something they'd never heard discussed. Many only saw their jobs as a form of tent-making (earning a living any way possible) in order to fund their "real" ministry of serving on church boards, teaching Sunday school, volunteering in local service projects, and going on short term mission trips. However, as the demands of their jobs grew, so did the level of frustration of their pastors, and their own sense of guilt for they had less and less time to volunteer in church activities.

> **Business can be done in ways that fulfill God's purposes *Intrinsically*—in the very work being done, and not just *Instrumentally*—as a means of income and witness to Christ.**

Some confessed that they didn't know how to wear their faith and their work at the same time. The *Second Vatican Council* of the Roman Catholic Church noted "the split between faith which many profess and their daily lives is one of the more serious errors of our age."[6]

---

[6] Second Vatican Council, Pastoral Constitution *Gaudium Et Spes* (1965), 43 cited in *Vocation of the Business Leader* (Pontifical Council for Justice and Peace, 2014), 6.
http://www.stthomas.edu/media/catholicstudies/center/johnaryaninstitute/publications/publicationpdfs/vocationofthebusinessleaderpdf/Pontifical Council_4.pdf

Some said that as businesspersons, when they walked through their church fellowship hall, they felt like a medieval leper and should ring a bell as they walked, warning others to get out of the way as they cried out "Unclean, Unclean." They felt that if fellow parishioners knew the compromises and moral bargains they made during the week, they would judge them as ungodly and unspiritual.

Their churches validate the Christian service of Sunday school teachers, youth workers, deacons and mission volunteers, but not the specific work of CEOs, judges, stockbrokers, store clerks, secretaries, or assembly line workers. The message was sent that these were secondary forms of Christian service—or rather—were really ways to support others who did the real work of ministry.

The traditional adage "if you can't go, then give, and if you can't give, then pray for those who've been sent," placed them on the sidelines of full-time Christian service. They were providers of much-needed resources for others to serve God, but they did not feel valued as frontline agents of the kingdom.

For Reflection and Discussion
How does this description of the typical ways churches validate "meaningful" work compare to your own experience?

3. The Dominant Emotions about Work
In light of the demands businesspersons feel at work, and the devaluation of their work they feel by their church, it is no wonder that many businesspersons feel unsupported and alone. The dominant emotions people felt (as reported in my small survey) as they were going to work in the morning, could be grouped around the following themes:

Fear of making a mistake, messing up a deal, being beaten by competitors, not making targets, or being found out for how incompetent they felt.

Loneliness because there was no one who really understood the challenges they faced at work to whom they could turn for counsel and support. Colleagues and supervisors were too risky. Friends and family members didn't fully grasp the business-issues. Church fellowship groups were primarily interested in personal, spiritual, and family life issues—not the challenges of business.

Envy for it seemed like other people had it better than they did—better jobs, better bosses, more success, or better skills.

These aren't the emotions any of us hoped would characterize our work life when we set out on our first job. Hopefully, they aren't what you feel. Out of 100 people I interviewed, only five indicated emotions of gratitude, contentment, and joy when they were anticipating their day at work. Surely it is not God's will that the majority of people live their lives feeling disengaged or even worse, hating their jobs. We long to feel joy, fulfillment, and gratitude about how we spend our days.

As a pastor, I have to realize that these are the everyday emotions of many of the people to whom I'm preaching on Sunday, engaged in committee meetings in the evening, and visiting in hospitals during the day. Has my preaching or pastoral care made any impact on this? If not, then my ministry is not touching dominant concerns in people's lives—concerns that also effect their family life, personal life, temptations, and fantasies. Merely to speak into their private spiritual life and public volunteer service is to leave untouched major areas of their life as followers of Christ.

For Reflection and Discussion

How does your description of the dominant emotions you feel at work relate to the previous summary of others' dominant emotions?

What is it about your experience at work that contributes to how you feel about it?

4. Responses to this Need

Fortunately, in recent decades there has been such a growing movement regarding a theology of business. For example, Seattle Pacific University's School of Business, Government, and Economics has focused on helping students understand "another way of doing business" that addresses the other "bottom-lines" God has for business, besides profit and share holder value. SPU's Seminary works with the university's Business School to offer combined degrees in Theology and Business.[7]

InterVarsity Christian Fellowship and numerous other associations around the world are focused on helping Christians in business see their work as a form of Christian service. For decades, Regent College in Vancouver, B.C. has offered courses and seminars for Christians in business. Fuller Theological Seminary's "Cascade Fellows" program, and the programs and resources of the Max De Pree Center for Leadership are also contributing to this movement of helping church leaders and businesspersons engage together around issues of work in the marketplace.[8]

Many local and national networks of Christians in business have emerged to provide forums to discuss how to do business from the perspective of the Christian faith. I've listed websites that provide helpful resources, insights and access to networks. Of special interest is "The Economic Wisdom Project," and the "Made to Flourish Pastors Network."[9] This network is breaking new ground in mobilizing pastors in their vision "to more effectively equip their congregations to better connect Sunday to Monday." Around the US, church leaders are joining regional networks and "witnessing a remarkable transformation in their congregations as they embrace a robust vocation and think integrally about how the Gospel speaks

---

[7] See www.spu.edu/academics/seattle-pacific-seminary/programs/dual-degrees/theology-and-business.

[8] See http://cascadefellows.com, http://depree.org.

[9] See www.economicwisdom.org, www.madetoflourish.org.

into every nook and cranny of life."[10] It is also encouraging to see ways church leaders are engaging for the first time with people in their congregations about the integration of business and faith through exploring together *Business as a Holy Calling?*

In the past twenty years, dozens of books have been written on a theology not just of work, but also specifically of business. Some of the themes in this study are developed more fully in Jeff Van Duzer's *Why Business Matters to God*; Kenman Wong and Scott Rae's book, *Business for the Common Good*; and Tom Nelson's, *Work Matters: Connecting Sunday Worship to Monday Work*. An excellent, concise summary of the rich insights of Catholic social teaching pertaining to business may be found in *Vocation of the Business Leader*. Greg Forster and others have created a concise summary of views by some evangelical theologians in *Twelve Elements of Economic Wisdom*. [11] A mutual fund company, Eventide Funds, has a full-time staff person focusing on the theology of business. Tim Weinhold's provocative blogs can be found at http://eventidefunds.com/faith-and-business/. Other helpful books and websites are listed in the Resource section.

The rapid growth of social entrepreneurship, the affirmations of corporate social responsibility, and more recently "B Corporations" express the growing recognition that business has a vital role in human well being that extends beyond profit and

We want all aspects of life on earth to participate in heaven coming to earth.

---

[10] Tom Nelson, President of Made to Flourish Pastors Network and author of *Work Matters: Connecting Sunday Worship* to MondayWork (Crossways, 2011).

[11] Jeff Van Duzer, *Why Business Matters to God and What Still Needs to Be Done to Fix It* (InterVarsity Press, 2010). Kenman Wong and Scott Rae, *Business for the Common Good: A Christian Vision for the Marketplace* (InterVarsity Press, 2011). *Vocation of the Business Leader* (Pontifical Council for Justice and Peace, 2014). *Twelve Elements of Economic Wisdom* (www.economicwisdom.org).

personal ambition. "B Corporations" are companies that are committed to create value for society and not just shareholders, and to using business as a force for good in the world. The "B" stands for "best for the world, and as of 2015 over 1,000 for-profit corporations have formally registered.[12] Ben & Jerry's and Patagonia are two examples of B Corporations.

5. Work as a Place for Radical Discipleship

Work has a significant impact on our lives and is central to how we engage with the world. It's interesting to note the comparatively small impact (at least in terms of hours) church and especially sermons have on our time (and maybe our values, views, and way of life). What has the most impact on our time, and where does our time have the most impact on our lives and world? Most people in the US spend over their lifetime:

> 254,000 hours **sleep** (if we are fortunate)
> 80,000 to 110,000 hours **work** (80,000 national average including part-time; 110,000 average full-time)
> 80,000 to 460,000 hours **view media**: TV, Internet, magazines (estimates widely vary depending on source)
> 48,000 hours **food** preparation, eating, cleaning up
> And particularly for Christians:
> 7,500 hours **church** activities
> 1,250 hours listen to **sermons**[13]

---

[12] "B Corps are certified by the non-profit B Lab to meet rigorous standards of social and environmental performance, accountability, and transparency." B Corp certification is parallel to "the good housekeeping seal of approval" or "fair trade certification" for those who embrace these values. For more information, a list of certified "B Corps," and an assessment tool that demonstrates the standards for certification, see http://www.bcorporation.net.

[13] Calculated as follows for the average American: Based on 79 year lifetime (2014) and 45 year work life:

Media: Statistics vary in extremes: *US Dept of Labor* indicates 3 hours/day of average media use; *Statista* indicates 11 to 18 hours/day depending on age = range of 80,000 to 460,000 life time hours (based on 75

No wonder we can easily be driven by desires, values, and visions that might be contrary to the kingdom of God. We want to work and live in ways that are consistent with God's purposes. Our prayer, *"Thy kingdom come, thy will be done on earth, as it is in heaven"* is as true for business as it is for churches, for marketing as it is for sermons. To participate in God's kingdom coming through business, we need intentional, specific, wise guidance for how to live our faith in complex business environments.

One implication of Jesus' kingdom prayer is an invitation for churches and church leaders to inspire in their parishioners a compelling vision of God's purposes for business. Sure, there is strain, struggle, and hardship in work. There is confusion, discouragement, and frustration. Business life is laden with temptations to take short cuts, to compromise integrity, to succumb to greed and ambition. That simply underscores all the more the vital importance of churches providing support for their businesspersons.

If we are praying for God's kingdom and will to come to earth as in heaven, then I doubt any church wants to leave its businesspersons feeling alone and even on their own, living their workday feeling fear, loneliness, and envy—or even hating their work. Paul says that the Kingdom of God is *"righteousness, peace, and joy in the Holy Spirit."*

---

years lifetime media use) www.bls.gov/news.release/pdf/atus.pdf;
    http://www.statista.com/statistics/276683/media-use-in-the-us/;
Sleep: 8.8 hours/day = 253,700 hrs over 79 years
Work: 47 hrs/week for full-time = 110,000 45 year work life;
    34.4 avg for all Americans including part-time = 80,000 total average.
    www.stats.oecd.org; Bureau of Labor Statistics, June 2015
    www.bls.gov/news.release/pdf/atus.pdf;
    www.washingtonpost.com/blogs/the-fix/wp/2015/07/09 ;.
Food: 1¾ hours/day (30 min/day eating) = 50,500 life time
    www.ers.usda.gov/media/149404/eib86.pdf.
Church: 3 hrs. /week
Sermons: 30 min/week

He prays that we be *"filled with all joy and hope in believing, so that we may abound in hope by the power of the Holy Spirit"* (Rom. 14:17; 15:13).

Central Questions: To deepen our vision and engagement in business as a holy calling, there are central questions to which we need answers:

- **Why would God call someone into business as their form of Christian service and ministry?**
- **How do we engage in business in ways that participate in God's will and ways?**
- **What would it look like for churches to structure their programs and purposes to equip and support Christians for ministry in business??**
- **What steps is God inviting me to take to engage in (or encourage) business as a way to participate in the coming of God's kingdom on earth?**

EXPANDING THE PURPOSES OF BUSINESS

In the biblical faith God invites us to earn our living (2 Thess. 3:10; Gal. 6:5-10). In fact, we're commanded to work and provide for our livelihood to the extent we're able. If you're making money you're not doing something that is ungodly. The issues God has with profit and with money pertain to why we're earning it, how we're doing it, and what we do with it. Paul completes the admonition for each to carry their own load in Gal. 6:5 with the admonition, *"let us work for the good of all"* (v. 10).

Unfortunately, sometimes the church has communicated an implicit disdain of profit as unspiritual. Many businesspersons suspect their pastors are "closet socialists" with a distrust of business for profit. This is reinforced in other religious traditions, such as Buddhism, in which priests are not supposed to "touch" money. It is spiritually unclean.

Let's be honest: for a business to make maximizing profit its reason for existence is to miss God's mark as seriously as it would be for a church to make maximizing donations in the Sunday offering its reason for existing. We would regard a church that existed to get donations as failing in its purposes. I propose that the same is true for a business that makes profit, income, or shareholder value its reason for existence. Biblically, the issue is why, how, and toward what end profit is gained.

I propose in this study that God's bottom line for business is deeper, richer, and more profound than mere profit. Profit and shareholder return on investment are essential and good. They are necessary for businesses to gain access to capital and to flourish. Profit is a good benchmark of a business' efficiency and value. But profit is merely an indicator and a means—not a purpose or goal.

Two Dominant Views of Profit

Profit is THE Goal	Profit is A Means
Milton Friedman: "[Some] businessmen believe that… business is not concerned 'merely' with profit but also with promoting desirable 'social' ends; that business has a 'social conscience' and takes seriously its responsibilities for providing employment, eliminating discrimination, avoiding pollution and whatever else may be the catch-words of the contemporary crop of reformers…Businessmen who talk this way are unwitting puppets of the intellectual forces that have been undermining the basis of a free society…In a free-	**Max Stackhouse:** "Profit is surely too limited a vision of management's ends. Profit is, in fact, only an indicator of whether or not the company is doing well in the short term. And every culture and every religion approves of profit if it does not in itself become the chief end of life, displacing all other ends, and if it contributes to the well being of the common-wealth. The larger task of business depends on its long-term ability to create the kinds and qualities of wealth that serve humanity and honor all that is holy."[15]

---

[15] Max Stackhouse, et al., *On Moral Business,* (Eerdmans, 1995), 27-28.

enterprise, private-property system a corporate executive is an employee of the owners of the business. He has direct responsibility to his employers. That responsibility is to conduct the business in accordance with their desires, which generally will be to make as much money as possible…"[14]

Shirley Roels: "Profits are also a measure of the effectiveness of our kingdom service. A lack of long-run profitability should cause us to ask important questions about our kingdom service. Are we being efficient in our use of resources? Are we being effective in meeting human needs?"[16]

For Reflection and Discussion

How do you evaluate these two depictions of profit?

To what extent have you sensed from the church that profit, or more generally, money itself, is somewhat "unclean"—except when it's given away?

How do you react to the assertion that profit is an essential *means* for business, but a very insufficient *end*?

Few businesses can survive without making a profit. Profit is normally essential. But that doesn't elevate it as *the* "bottom bottom-line"—the one primary purpose of business. Businesses have opportunities to contribute to the well being of society and the flourishing of creation in areas that church ministries, mission agencies, or other non-profit organizations can seldom reach. Government foreign aid, and the fruitful work of development agencies make vital and good contributions.

The economic impact of non-profit organizations on those in poverty is essential, but minor, compared to the impact of business

---

[14] Milton Friedman, "The Social Responsibility of Business is to Increase its Profits" *NY Times Magazine*, 13 Sept. 1970, pp. 32-33.

[16] Shirley Roels, *On Moral Business*, 912.

on our way of life, and on raising people out of poverty.[17] In 2015, due to the impact of education, health care, business development, and social safety nets, the number of people in the world living in extreme poverty has dropped to under 10%. The President of the World Bank, Jim Yong Kim described this as "the best story in the world today—these projections show us that we are the first generation in human history that can end extreme poverty."[18]

An article in Fortune Magazine illustrates the profound impact of business on the world, "27 companies that have changed the world." Their top 6 include:

1. Standard Oil that was the umbrella for John D. Rockefeller's petroleum monopoly until it was broken up in 1911—which led the way for gas and oil being the driving force of our lifestyle, economic change (and possibly climate change).

2. AT&T that not only led the way for electronic communication, but also the transistor.

3. McCormick Harvesting Machine Co. that brought the industrial revolution to agriculture.

4. G.D. Searle, inventors of the first birth control pill in 1957.

5. Ford that led the way in assembly line production, accessible transportation, and increased workers wages.

---

[17] For more on this see http://www.povertycure.org/issues/enterprise-solutions-to-poverty/, http://www.centerforfinancialinclusion.org, Michael Fairbanks, et. al. *In the River They Swim: Essays from Around the World on Enterprise Solutions to Poverty* (Templeton Press, 2009) and *Plowing the Sea: Nurturing the Hidden Sources of Growth in the Developing World* (Harvard Business Review Press, 1997), and Peter Greer, *Entrepreneurship for Human Flourishing* (Values and Capitalism) (AEI Press, 2014).

[18] http://www.worldbank.org/en/news/press-release/2015/10/04/world-bank-forecasts-global-poverty-to-fall-below-10-for-first-time-major-hurdles-remain-in-goal-to-end-poverty-by-2030

6. British East India Company that was the driving force behind the British Empire and at one point controlled half the world's trade.[19]

Based on the assumption that God has additional purposes for business besides making money and ensuring a profit, what are they? To what extent can these purposes be regarded as intrinsic to the purpose of business, and not just good and desirable side benefits—or secondary objectives? This study is structured around six additional "bottom lines" for business in addition to profit. Each section in this study will focus on one of these additional bottom-lines for business.

1. **Profit**
2. **Community:** Does a business build positive, caring human relationships in ways that honor as well as bridge differences?
3. **Work and Wages:** Does our business treat and pay employees fairly, provide meaningful work and contribute to the provision for legitimate human needs?
4. **Stewardship:** Does a particular business endeavor steward people, capital, natural resources, and the environment in ways that honor God's will and ways?
5. **Justice:** Are people—employees, customers and competitors—treated with dignity in ways that contribute to life being made right?
6. **Integrity:** Are qualities of honesty, kindness, diligence, and service nurtured in the characters of all who are affected by this business?
7. **Creativity:** Is creation guarded, ordered and rendered more fruitful, innovation encouraged, and creative responses developed for products, services, and a work environment that

---

[19] "27 Companies that Changed the World," *Fortune Magazine.* June 11, 2014. http://fortune.com/2014/06/11/27-companies-that-changed-the-world/

satisfy legitimate human needs and contribute to people (and nature) flourishing?

Rather than merely one "bottom-line" for business—profit and maximizing shareholder value; or even three—profit, stakeholder value, and care of creation; this study proposes seven. Regardless of whether or not the owners, managers, or workers in a business are Christian, I propose that these bottom-lines are consistent with God's revealed purposes for all businesses.

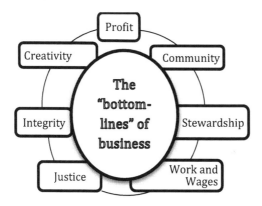

Why list "bottom lines" as a circle? They are interdependent. Profit is essential if there is to be money to nourish community with all stakeholders, pay good wages, attract and develop good staff, pay the extra costs of guarding creation and working towards justice in society, doing the right thing to build integrity even if it costs, and investing in creativity.

The importance of profit doesn't necessarily make it the bottom "bottom-line." The assertion in this study is that growing in fulfillment of the other six is equally essential for business. Is a business worth doing if it has a destructive impact on human lives and community? If working conditions and wages don't contribute to people's well being then isn't a business contrary to God's purposes? Unless creation, time, and money are stewarded then won't justice and integrity in society be diminished? Unless creativity is encouraged, it's likely that business will languish, profit will decline, and morale will deteriorate.

These bottom-line purposes of business can be portrayed on a continuum, for all businesses are at varying points in fulfilling them. At the end of each section, participants will be given the opportunity to conduct a personal "audit" that will examine the connection of their specific business, and their role in it, to these purposes of God—and develop personal strategies for moving their business toward greater alignment with God's purposes in each of the bottom-lines.

Businesses that move toward contributing to each one of these "bottom-lines" will be fruitful expressions of God's will and ways for human life. They will contribute to human spirits and bodies flourishing—rather than, as Terkel says, experiencing violence. As we explore the importance of business in the purposes of God, we will find ourselves appreciating more and more business as a holy calling.

Bottom-Lines and Balanced Scorecards

Some readers have confused "bottom-lines" with "balanced scorecards." I don't believe they address the same topic. Half of all businesses in the Western world employ a very helpful "balanced scorecard" management and strategic planning tool.[20] A common scorecard evaluates how four factors—financial performance and stewardship, efficient internal business processes, innovation, and stakeholder satisfaction—contribute to fulfilling the organization's mission, vision, and strategy. Key performance measures are developed to assess each area.

---

[20] See Robert Kaplan and David Norton, "Using the Balanced Scorecard as a Strategic Management System," *Harvard Business Review* (Jan-Feb 1996), 76. For more see http://www.balancedscorecard.org.

The bottom-lines proposed in this study ask a different set of questions than those examined in a "balanced scorecard" and "key performance indicators." Scorecards and indicators focus on how well we do what we do in business. They focus on performance. Bottom-lines focus on *why* we do what we do and how closely this aligns with the purposes of God. When we see and strengthen the connection between our business—and our specific work within it—and God's purposes, our sense of meaning, value, and fulfillment deepens.

The Importance of Knowing Our Purpose

Victor Frankl, a psychiatrist who survived the Holocaust, stressed that a sense of purpose is integral to human flourishing. A sense of meaning and purpose sustained people through the atrocities of the concentration camp. [21] This

A person with a solid enough WHY can endure nearly any WHAT.

isn't meant to compare business to concentration camps. Rather, it underscores how essential a deep sense of purpose is for flourishing, and even for survival. If we see a solid and significant purpose to our business beyond survival (making a living or even getting rich). Without a grand WHY, we are likely to focus on HOW—ethics, and WHAT—methods. As a result, we will easily be co-opted by the values and methods of the system in which we serve. Every business and job has its own rewards and punishments to encourage behavior that conforms to its norms and penalize those that do not. Thus, all the indicators might tell us we are succeeding, yet we might be missing out on the joy of knowing our business contributes to God's kingdom coming and will being done here, now, on earth—as it is in heaven.

---

[21] Victor Frankl, *Man's Search for Meaning* (Buchaneer Books, 1959).

Holy work can be done joyfully. Work in business needn't be the wearisome grind of daily life. God's Spirit wants to lift our lives into the rhythm of God's ways. We want to end each day, and reach the end of our days, with the contented affirmation, "It's been good. By God's grace and strength I was able to live much of my life in harmony with the purposes of God." We don't merely succumb to the struggles and temptations of the established way of doing business. Nor do we merely decorate the edges of our lives with activities that are meaningfully "Christian."

Connecting our work to the purposes of God

The more we can see connection between our business and God's purposes, the greater will be our joy and contentment. The more business participates in the purposes of God, the more it can be **"Business is a noble calling, provided…"** done as a "holy calling." Pope Francis calls business "a noble vocation, provided that those engaged in it see themselves challenged by a greater meaning in life; this will enable them to serve the common good by striving to increase the goods of this world and to make them more accessible to all."[22]

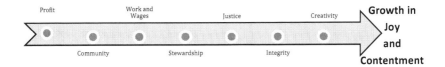

Business as a holy calling is rooted in utter confidence in God's will for all people to abound and that business has a vital role in this.

"May the God of hope fill you with all joy and peace in believing so that you may abound in hope by the power of the Holy Spirit" (Rom 15:13). *Abound*

---

[22] Pope Francis, Apostolic Exhortation *Evangeli Gaudium* (2013), 203; cited in *Vocation of the Business Leader* .5.

means "to overflow." God's will is for our lives to overflow with joy, peace, and hope.

For Reflection and Discussion
What would you like to learn and to receive in order to answer the questions about faith and business listed on pages 27-28 with confidence that business is done in ways that are consistent with God's purposes?

In order to view my work (and especially business) as a form of Christian service, I need to understand the following more fully:

If my church is to engage in and support the work life of its members, I need to gain more insight into:

By the end of this study, I hope to be better able to:

At the end of this entire study, you will be invited to revisit your answers to these questions. This will both indicate the extent to which your hopes and expectations have been met—as well as clarify possible next steps you and your church might want to take.

2. COMMUNITY: SURROUNDED BY THE SACRED

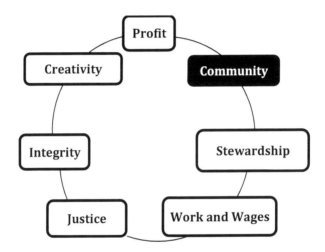

This section asserts that every business activity touches that which is sacred, regardless of the religious beliefs of the businessperson.

By the end, participants should be able to summarize what they can do to nourish relationships at work that encourage community well being.

CENTRAL QUESTION: How does the notion that every business decision is a theological decision and everything done in business relates to God (whether we know it or not) impact your attitude toward business?

Some might think this is a strange place to begin a discussion of God's purposes or bottom-lines for business. Shouldn't we begin with issues of work and money? Though it might make sense to begin with chapter three—work, wages, and stewardship—my conviction is that God's purposes begin at a different point.

We are created in the image of God and the Christian faith affirms that God exists in triune relationships of love—Father, Son, and Spirit. As image bearers of the "relational" God, we are wise to begin with God's relational nature and purposes. We are most fully ourselves when we live in supportive, inclusive, diverse relationships. We are created for life in community—common unity. With 100,000 lifetime hours spent there, the workplace is one of the most obvious venues for experiencing community.

Consider the following story: She wanted to do her work to the glory of God, but was not sure what that meant. Surely, that meant caring for people and somehow witnessing to her faith. However, by the time she arrived at work to clean the office building, everyone had gone home for the day. She decided that, at least, she could do her work well. That would please God. So she cleaned the office until it glistened. But was there more? After a few weeks she decided that as she cleaned she could pray for people in the office. She'd pray for the people whose pictures were on the desk, asking that they would be refreshed and encouraged, and that the employee would be able to return to work in the morning ready for a new day. Seeking more ways to serve, she decided to write one person a note at the end of each day: *"Dear _____ I hope you had a refreshing evening and that you are blessed as you come to work tomorrow. Love, the Cleaning Lady."*

After several months of this, she came to work one night, hung up her coat and pulled her cleaning cart out of the closet. Just as she was setting to work she was surprised as everyone jumped up from behind their desks, wheeling out a cart with cake and punch. "We had to meet you," they said. "We'd all noticed how the atmosphere in our office changed over the past months. We were getting along better, doing better work, and even our customers commented about the changes. We couldn't figure it out—until we all started sharing the unusual notes we were getting. Perhaps you are the cause and we all wanted to meet you and thank you."

DOING BUSINESS ON HOLY GROUND

Business is about more than creating work and making money. Yes, the provision of a sustainable livelihood, enabling meaningful work, and even making a profit are integral to the purposes of business. But, if we begin or end there in our understanding, and we miss out on the depth and breadth of God's purposes for—and even delight in—business.

1. Every Business Decision is a Theological Decision.

Years ago a Christian friend who is a successful businessperson invited me to a meeting of several Jewish business leaders, a rabbi and the chief economic officer of the Bank of Israel. Our purpose was to discuss differences between Christian and Jewish approaches to business. These Jewish leaders' ability to discuss the theological implications of business issues was stunning. If they didn't have an answer, they would turn to their rabbi for theological reasoning on issues such as minimum wage legislation, international trade treaties and regulations, and government subsidies of particular industries.

Neither my Christian friend nor I had ever looked at these issues theologically, nor would he ever dream of approaching his pastor to learn the "correct" answer. My friend mused, "Why would I do that? What would my pastor know about my business?" But for these Jewish leaders, every business issue was a theological issue.[23]

2. Business is Surrounded by the Sacred

Wherever a businessperson turns, and whatever is done—business is dealing with that which is sacred to God.

The Name and Glory of God	People in the Image of God
BUSINESS	
Resources that Belong to God	Time that is Ordered by God

People are in the Image of God. All people are sacred. People are to be treated with dignity and a sense of wonder. C. S. Lewis made an insightful observation that next to Holy Communion, the most "sacred thing" we ever encounter on earth is the person seated next to us. As image-bearers of God, there are no "ordinary" people.[24] Everyone is a person of indescribable worth, regardless of financial situation. Lewis noted

> There are no "ordinary" people. Everyone we encounter is to be treated as someone of extraordinary worth.

that we are en route to becoming creatures of unimaginable beauty and splendor such that if we saw one another now as we one day will be; we would fall on our knees in reverent awe. Or we take an opposite journey, becoming hideous creatures such as those we encounter only in our worst nightmares. How we treat one another contributes towards what we are becoming.

---

[23] For an excellent summary of the Hebrew Bible's teaching on business, see Hershey H. Friedman, "Creating a Company Code of Ethics: Using the Bible as a Guide." *Electronic Journal of Business Ethics and Organization Studies*, Vol. 8 (1), April 2003.

[24] C.S. Lewis, *The Weight of Glory and Other Essays* (Harper, 2001), 45-46.

An interesting example of treating others with care comes, of all places, from the mining industry. Mining is unavoidably a rough and tumble industry that has very narrow financial margins. Companies are continually looking for ways to reduce costs and increase productivity. It's usually thought of as a hard-driving business that places high demands on workers. Yet for many mining companies, no meeting would dare begin without everyone first engaging in a time of "safety sharing." At the beginning of a meeting (whether of mine laborers, management executives, or even board members) everyone shares safety concerns or insights. These obviously begin with the work site, but they can extend to after work issues: "It's really stormy today so be careful driving home." "Does everyone have their cars equipped with winter driving survival kits?" "Make sure if you're outdoors this weekend, use sunscreen and wear a hat (if it's summer)," or "be careful if you're up on a ladder installing Christmas lights." The commitment to the well being of workers extends to every aspect of their safety with the goal of zero accidents or injuries, at any time, among their work force.[25]

For Reflection and Discussion

How might our interactions be impacted if we treated people knowing that those with whom we work, from whom we buy goods and services, to whom we market, and with whom we compete are sacred—creatures in the image of God?

How do I treat others as "sacred" when they are manipulative, exploitive, corrupt, or otherwise untrustworthy?

Resources belong to God. Time is ordered by God. Money, time, and natural resources are sacred. *"The earth with all that is in it belongs to the Lord"* (Ps. 24:1). We will explore the implications of this truth in subsequent sections. It can reshape our approach to money, possessions, people, and creation. Through many parables about tax

---

[25] For more information about this see http://www.safetyshare.org.

collectors or the tenants in the master's vineyard, Jesus drives home the point that our resources are not our own. As Paul reminds us in 1 Cor. 4:7: *"What do you have that you did not receive?"* Is not everything we have a gift from God? In business, we are not asking people to use "their" resources

We are not owners of anything. We are stewards of someone else's possessions.

to buy "our" goods and services. We are giving people an opportunity to partner with us in stewarding God's resources according to God's will and ways. Together we seek to promote the common good—the flourishing of people and of creation.[26]

God's commitment to "community" includes all people—and all of creation. God's will is for all people and all of creation to flourish in life-giving harmony. The Hebrew word for this is "shalom." Practices that contribute to this are consistent with God's will and ways. Practices that thwart this aren't. God owns all and all bear the mark of God's creativity. Business touches God's deep concerns, for it deals with money, people, and the resources of time and the material creation.

For Reflection and Discussion

How might our approach to resources be impacted if we treated the material things we consume (and waste), the money we seek (and squander), and the time we use (and frivol away) as not our own but belonging to God?

3. The value of business is shaped by purposes not finances.

What occurs in and through a business can't help but be of deep concern to God—since business is dealing with people and

---

[26] See Kenman Wong and Scott Rae, *Business for the Common Good: A Christian Vision for the Marketplace* (IVP Academic, 2011), and Timothy Keller, *Every Good Endeavor: Connecting Your Work to God's Work* (Riverhead Books, 2014).

resources made by God. Because business is close to God's heart, God belongs at the heart of business.

What a society consumes gives a sense of what it values and needs. Few Western cities can match Accra, Ghana for having streets dotted with businesses marketing elaborate, colorful coffins. AIDS impacts business. Few billboards in Western cities advertise skin-lightening products such as are found throughout Asia. Few Muslim cities tolerate billboards with scantily clad models marketing perfume or fashion. Sometimes, business provokes desires for things people didn't know they either wanted or needed, and then business promotes products that purportedly satisfy those longings. A society's ads disclose some of what it thinks it needs and values.

Because we are surrounded by the sacred, anytime someone is provoking desires and dealing with human need they are engaged in something that is "spiritually charged." It is not "merely" secular, or irrelevant to God. Rather, God is very much present, engaged in, and "concerned" with what needs are being met, what desires are being provoked, and what values are being expressed.

God values all people and all creation. *God hears the cries of all human needs and of all creation (Romans 8).*

One purpose of business is to respond to these needs *by providing goods and services that contribute to people and creation flourishing in community.*

TEMPTATIONS, DISTRACTIONS, AND OPPOSITION

Because of the central importance of business in God's purposes, it's not surprising that also found at the heart of business is the adversary of God. Business is a deeply spiritual vocation, engaging both with God's purposes for humankind, and with powers and principalities—demonic forces that seek to thwart the fulfillment of those purposes. We are continually tempted to turn in on ourselves, relying only on our finances, our abilities, and ourselves. We can easily become captivated by our own needs, ambitions, and desires—or by others' selfishness. We can become controlled by the demands of our circumstances. We can lose all regard for God or awareness that we are engaged in creating life-giving community.

1. Wearing More than Our Work Clothes

People in business face particular temptations as well as opportunities to influence human life, human societies, and all of creation for good or ill. Businesses can express and indeed further the ravages of sin or contribute to the redeeming purposes of God. Business engages directly with the deepest human temptations toward greed and idolatry—power, money, and reliance on our own efforts and resources for survival and status—and the deepest longings for well-being and flourishing. Therefore, every business decision contributes to our being diverted from the will and way of God—or contributes to God's good purposes. Unfortunately, too many Christians confess that they don't know how to wear their faith and their business clothes at the same time.

It's essential for Christians in business to be clothed in Christ and wear the "armor of God" (Eph 6:10-18; Col 2:6). Lest we think of this only in combative terms, Paul reminds us, *"Clothe yourselves with compassion, humility, meekness, and patience...Above all, clothe yourselves with love"* (Col 3.12, 14). The Adversary seeks to thwart human well-being. In business we are on a front-line in the encounter between the purposes of God and the thrashing about of the Adversary, for we are engaged with how people gain access to the resources necessary for them to flourish. To engage in business is to enter into arenas of spiritual combat for we are face to face to issues of what we worship, what we trust, and in what we find our identity and worth.

The Adversary can use business to turn people in upon themselves.	The Spirit can use business to turn us outward toward caring for others.
The Adversary can use business to	The Spirit can use business to guard

trap us in trusting our own labor to secure our livelihood.	and nourish all creation.
The Adversary can use business to tempt us to live as if we were our own gods.	The Spirit can use business to contribute to the world being made right.

Because of the ways the Adversary can distract businesses, and because of the central importance of business in God's purposes, churches are wise to devote focused corporate intercessory prayer for their businesspersons. That for which a church prays gives a strong indicator of what it regards as important. We'll pray about our church finances, but not for the financial management of corporations that can shape entire economies. We'll pray for people to recover from illness but forget to intercede for our entire healthcare system, or for sick economies.

How ironic that we'll commission people in prayer to go on short-term mission trips, but never think of commissioning real estate developers or construction workers for their ministry in daily life. Years ago I had a fascinating conversation over several months with an earnest Christian friend who just couldn't believe that it was ok to pray about his business issues. "Surely God isn't interested in and has far more pressing concerns to deal with than my marketing strategies and cash flow problems." As we explored together both the nature of God's goodness, and the nature of his business issues, his faith lit up with earnest prayer for his business.

2. Commissioning All People for All of Life

What might be the impact on the quality of community care in our church life, and in our city and neighborhood, if during a series of church worship services we commissioned everyone in the church for their ministry in daily life?

- Each Sunday someone representing a particular vocational category could give a testimony regarding the challenges and opportunities he or she faced serving God in their work.

- Then everyone involved in a similar form of work could be invited to stand before the congregation and have hands laid on them, as people prayed for their ministry.
- Sunday after Sunday different groups could be commissioned (business related, as well as other forms of service): education, parenting, health care, construction and building trades, finance and accounting, real estate, marketing, computer and software development, aerospace, scientific and medical research, government, social service, the police and judicial systems, military, elder care, child care, volunteer service, gardening and landscape, forestry, fisheries, art, media and communication, journalism, etc.
- Not only might this highlight and affirm the value of their work as Christian ministry, it could also help nurture affinity groups as people discovered others in similar occupations.

In the congregation I served as a pastor, we tried a modified version of this. As a result, many groups started meeting for prayer, to discuss responses to common issues, and to provide mutual support. Some groups are still meeting, twenty-years later. New networks of Christian businesspersons were formed which continue to meet. A group of members involved in the criminal justice system started meeting to explore the meaning and implications of biblical justice for their work—and is still meeting, 25 years later.

3. Prayer and Business
People in business are aware of—and can pray for—needs, wounds, temptations, and opportunities in our world that might normally never be mentioned in Sunday morning worship.
- Do we as a church intercede for people as they make business-related financial decisions, asking that these resources be stewarded well, and that good things will happen in society and in creation as a result?
- Are we praying for people making decisions about employment, the development of products, the provoking of desire through

advertising and marketing, the designing of buildings and roads, water supplies, and sewer systems? The Anglican Prayer Book has a blessing for sewage treatment plants!

- We pray for those in our congregations who are unemployed to get work—but do we pray for our businesses and economy to flourish and generate meaningful jobs?

- We pray for individual's health and medical needs—but do we regularly intercede for health care workers whose skill and decisions have an impact people's health? Do we pray for the economic issues involved in health insurance and the ability of people to pay for treatment?

For Reflection and Discussion

In what ways do you incorporate these dimensions of prayer into your prayer for business, and for businesspersons in your congregation?

1. We ask God to show us how God is present and what God is doing in our place of work, how we can honor God in all that we do, and how we can participate in what God is doing.

2. We pray for the Spirit to alter the atmosphere of our business, so that it becomes a place of kindness and care, fruitfulness and significance for the kingdom.

3. We pray for wisdom, courage, and love so that we treat everyone we encounter with dignity and respect.

4. We pray to be responsible in how we secure and use resources, and not to be distracted and diverted into the pursuit of frivolous projects that squander our time and the earth's resources.

5. We ask for protection and wisdom in response to specific ethical issues we face that day, and pray the same for our co-workers, our supervisors, our competitors, suppliers, and customers.

6. We pray for protection from the forces of evil that seek to defile our credibility and distort our approach to money and resources.

7. We review, at each day's end, what we saw God doing that day, how we missed out on being aware of God's presence, or how we had the joy of participating in it, and how we could have lived more faithfully and fruitfully.

After attending a *Business as a Holy Calling?* group, Carl decided for the first time to pray for his work in a financial services firm. He found another Christian in the office and they met early to pray for business issues, for staff relations, and for difficult issues with customers. He reported that Wednesdays (their day of prayer) have become the best day of the week. Strained relationships are eased, customers seem more satisfied, and guidance "appears" for response to complex financial decisions. It had never occurred to him before that God would actually be interested in and engage with a financial services business.

Bernie works as one member of a design team at Boeing. Convinced that God is the Creator, and that God is interested in all aspects of life, Bernie prays silently throughout the day for the projects he's working on. He asks the Lord for specific guidance on how to solve a particular design problem. Insights suddenly come to him, and as a result, through innovative, never-before-imagined inventions in the design process, he has gained over a half dozen patents for his team.

Lisa, another participant in a *Business as a Holy Calling?* group, has teamed up with several friends and they are invited by Christians in business to come visit them at work and pray with them for the business, issues the business is facing, and faithfulness to God's purposes for the business.

For Reflection and Discussion
What would it look like if in your church service, the prayers of intercession focused more on the business issues faced by people in your congregation?

What's been your experience praying for business-related issues?

49

BUSINESS REQUIRES CONTINUAL CONVERSION

Special emphasis must be placed on the spirituality of our businesspersons and of their business activities. Martin Luther is often quoted as saying, "There are three conversions necessary: the conversion of the heart, mind, and the purse."[27] Charles Spurgeon preached that, "With some, the last part of their nature that ever gets sanctified is their pockets."[28] When we design advertising and marketing campaigns, manufacture products, and market services, we are wise to be conscious of:

- whom we are serving,
- what we are seeking,
- what desires and emotions we are provoking, and even
- what we are worshipping.

We need God's Spirit to "convert" us every day, not just to "save our souls" but also to redeem every aspect of our lives.

We need moment by moment conversion *from* being consumed by our needs, desires, and ambitions		*To* living in Christ and participating in God's love for others.
We need moment by moment conversion *from* focusing only on gaining and guarding our own resources		*To* trusting God with all things and stewarding them in ways consistent with God's purposes.

[27] There is no documentation in Luther's writings of this statement. Richard Foster quotes it in *Money, Sex, and Power* (Harper Collins,1985),9. Scott Rodin develops it into a novel on money, *The Third Conversion* (Kingdom Life Publishing, 2011). Luther did comment that by God's grace, when someone repents, one is "transformed into another man [sic] with another heart, another disposition, another mind, and another life." He "must tie the best form of repentance to his own purse." *Defense and Explanation of All the Articles* (1521), vol. 32, p. 39.

[28] Charles Spurgeon, The Metropolitan Tabernacle Pulpit, *Sermons,* vol.14.xlviii.

We need moment by moment conversion *from* conforming to society's measures of worth, significance, and success *To* finding our identity and worth as beloved sons and daughters of God.

We need a conversion—a radical change in our way of living—so that we can live the *"good, perfect, and acceptable will of God"* (Romans 12:2).

For Reflection and Discussion

How does the assertion that we are surrounded by the sacred in business strike you?

- In what ways does this seem strange and impossible?

- In what ways does it feel like an invitation?

- How might you engage in your work differently if you lived with this perspective?

Discuss and reflect on how you might pray for your business and for your involvement in it.

Personal Strategies for Catalyzing Change. What do I sense God is calling me to do within my sphere of responsibilities and influence to enhance community?

1. Community	Strategies for catalyzing change
Interests: How do I feel called to enhance the quality of community in my workplace?	
Sphere of responsibility: How can my role contribute to this?	
Ways to model the change I value: What can I do immediately?	
Concerns outside my responsibility: What issues and opportunities relating to community are outside my role?	
Key people: How can I build key relationships to encourage and support others in their spheres of responsibility (in areas about which I'm concerned)?	
Prayer: For what can I pray?	

If you want to evaluate this and strategize your response further, see *Evaluating How My Business and Work Participate in God's Purposes*

3. STEWARDSHIP OF TIME AND MONEY: YOUR BUSINESS IS GOD'S BUSINESS

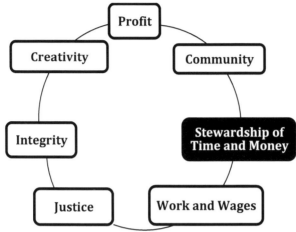

This section examines the proposal that an "economic system" (how a society organizes the exchange of goods and services, and the allocation of resources) is outlined in the Bible and explores its relevance for our modern economies.

By the end, participants should understand some of the components of biblical teaching about the economy, and evaluate the applicability of these teachings for our contemporary contexts.

CENTRAL QUESTIONS: Does the assertion that an economic system is outlined in the Bible surprise you? What's your response to the suggestions of ways this is relevant in our contemporary economy?

A Biblical Economic System?

Some people are surprised by the notion that an economic system to organize the exchange of goods and services, and the allocation of resources, is outlined in the Bible. Surely the Bible is more concerned with spirituality than business plans, more with worship services than corporate investment portfolios!

Pope Francis' declarations about business and encyclical about the environment have provoked some devout Catholic politicians to declare that the Church should stick to religion and stay out of areas of science and business where it has no expertise. For example, Rick Santorum declared, "I think we probably are better off leaving science to the scientists and we [the church] should focus on what it's good at, which is theology and morality." Jeb Bush declared, "I don't get my economic policy from my bishops or my cardinals or my pope."[29]

The Old Testament theologian Walter Brueggemann comments, "Christians have a long history of trying to squeeze Jesus out of public life and reduce him to a private little Savior…Many people, both inside and outside of the church, haven't a clue that Jesus is [often] talking about the economy…Our world absolutely requires this news. It has nothing to do with being Republicans or Democrats, liberals or conservatives, socialists or capitalists. It is much more elemental: the creation is infused with the Creator's generosity, and we can find practices, procedures, and institutions that allow that generosity to work."[30]

---

[29] Pope Francis, *Laudato Si*. For Catholic politicians' responses see *Time Magazine* June 17, 2015.

[30] Walter Brueggemann, "The Liturgy of Abundance, the Myth of Scarcity," *Christian Century* (Vol 116. No. 10, March 24, 1999). www.religion-online.org/showarticle.sasp/title:533.

It shouldn't surprise us that God would have specific guidance about not just the process by which we do business (business ethics), but the purposes it serves. History makes it undeniably evident that how we organize the exchange of goods and services, and how we allocate resources can have a profoundly positive or a tragically negative impact on human life and creation. It is possible to succeed in a business that is built on the wrong purposes. We might pray for the success and protection of a business, without being aware of or paying attention to ways it violates the sacredness of life. We can so separate our spiritual life from our business practices, and so focus on the rewards found through succeeding according to the "rules" of our business—that we are blinded to the reality and implications of what we are doing.

I experienced this vividly one day on a trip to Senegal. The dungeons of the Goree Island, Senegal slave fort led to the "door of no return"—a narrow passageway to the waiting ships, through which passed hundreds of thousands of the fifteen million African men, women and children who were sold as slaves to the new world from 1502-1860s. Above the dungeons, the slave traders had built their chapel. I doubt their organ music and hymns of praise to Jesus could drown out the cries of the captives below. Somehow they managed their devotion to God in ways that permitted them to rationalize biblical teaching that challenged the hideous purposes that shaped their entire business, and indeed, built much of our Western economy. Arguments in favor of traffic in humans as commodities often included the obvious fact that the Western economy and lifestyle depended on it. To stop slavery would lead to economic collapse. Several provocative books that document the economic significance of slavery for Western economies have been published recently.[31]

---

[31] For a two minute overview of the history of the Atlantic slave trade see, http://www.slate.com/articles/life/the_history_of_american_slavery /2015/06/animated_interactive_of_the_history_of_the_atlantic_slav

What does this tragic history have to do with the contemporary purpose of business? Besides the fact that much of our Western economy was built on the backs of slave labor for several hundred years, and other than possible (but unlikely) reparations for their descendants, is there any other relevance to the Goree Island slave fort for today?

As I sat in that chapel, imagining how it provided sanctuary for the traders and justified (in their mind) the suffering of the trafficked—I wondered, over what "slave dungeons" am I worshiping today?

- How have I deafened myself to the injustices and evils upon which my lifestyle is built?
- Are there ways I've constructed religious beliefs, found biblical proof texts, and institutionalized social practices that justify this, and blind me to how my economic decisions thwart God's good purposes for all people?
- Am I fearful that aligning our business practices with all of God's bottom-lines might threaten my lifestyle and income?
- Am I unwilling to consider these issues because I fear facing them would jeopardize our profitability?
- What are the supply chain implications for the places we source the materials for our products, our purchases, or for where we dispose of by-products and waste?

Beyond all these possibly indirect issues, there are the harsh facts that somewhere between 21 and 33 million people today work as slaves. Their average cost to purchase is only $90 (compared to $40,000 in 1809 adjusted to today's currency). For example, it is

---

e_trade.html. For the history of the relationship of slavery to the American and Western economies, see the recent works by Edward Baptist, *The Half Has Never Been Told: Slavery and the Making of American Capitalism* (Basic Books, 2014), and Sven Beckert, *The Empire of Cotton: A Global History* (Knopf, 2014).

estimated that 90% of all shrimp imported into the U.S. relies on some form of bonded or forced labor to produce it.[32]

There is a disturbing survey that estimates the number of people who are in slavery producing the products we consume (http://www.slaveryfootprint.org.) I completed their questionnaire and it produced the stunning estimate that I rely on the slave labor of over 60 people![33] Whether or not this "slavery calculator" is 100% accurate, it points to a sobering reality in our present world. Though I don't have any personal, domestic servants to wait on me. I rely on the servant (if not slave) labor of dozens of unseen workers.

For Reflection and Discussion

What, if anything, do you think is the pertinence of this extreme, and emotionally painful example of slavery for our current discussion of business as a holy calling?

How do you respond to this?

What questions does this raise for you regarding the "supply side" sourcing of resources used in your business, or for that matter, your own personal consumption?

Some assert that it's too overwhelming to even consider these issues. Others that their business would be uncompetitive and their personal lifestyle too expensive if they only relied on ethically sourced products. What are your thoughts about this?

---

[32] For statistics and further analysis see http://www.endslaverynow.org.
[33]

THE FOUNDATIONS OF BIBLICAL ECONOMICS

Rather than being paralyzed by the complexity of these issues, I believe we are invited to trust that God has a will and a way forward for us. The Bible contains specific commands regarding God's will for business, economics, and money. Though the biblical injunctions were given to agrarian, localized economies with face-to-face, community-based exchanges, they carry clear implications for business in today's market economies.

If we limit the Bible to a devotional book, we may limit its economic wisdom for contemporary business

1. Business as Stewardship

Work, and by implication we can suggest business, were part of God's good creation—not the consequence of the human Fall. In the beginning of the Bible God outlines some of the foundations for a system for distributing goods and services and allocating resources. One of God's first interactions with the earliest man and woman, according to the book of Genesis 1-3, was to assign and honor productive work. Human labor is given a significant role in the purposes of God.

Work is a form of creative stewardship through which we:

- Carefully manage the rest of creation (Gen. 1:26, 28),
- Order it (name it) (Gen 2:19-20),
- Protect and guard it (Gen 2:15),
- Render it fruitful (Gen 1:28; 2:15).

Some people's notions of dominion and of God's absolute sovereignty have led to a more exploitive view of how people use natural resources. Calvin Beisner, for example, suggests that any notion of climate change is a distortion by environmentalists and expresses lack of trust in God. He asserts that unalterable, human-caused destruction of the environmental can't happen. God "foresaw all that mankind could ever do, and made the world fit to sustain us as long as He intends us to be here."[34] If we make the earth no longer livable for humans, it is because then is the time God wants to usher in the new heaven and earth.

We propose a different understanding of stewardship. A good steward is someone who carefully and responsibly manages someone else's resources that the owner has entrusted into their care. Humans are called to steward creation by "taming" the "garden," and by exercising "dominion" over creation in Genesis 1:26 and 28 in the same ways that God exercises dominion—through grace, love, and care in order to liberate—rather than to dominate. Thus in Genesis 2:15 we are called to guard creation and help it be fruitful. Adam is placed in the garden to "keep" and "care for" it. This is dominion by wise, careful stewardship. Unfortunately an exclusive focus on "dominion" as domination has often been used to justify people's exploitation rather than protection of creation.

> "The Bible starts out with a liturgy of abundance...The real issue confronting us is whether the news of God's abundance can be trusted in the face of the story of scarcity."
> Walter Brueggemann

The Bible begins with affirmations that:

- God created all of life and all things exist by God's will (without being themselves god).

- God's original creation was good and harmonious;

---

[34]Calvin Beisner, Prospects of Growth: A Biblical View of Population, Resources and the Future (Crossway, 1990), 153. James Watt, US Secretary of the Interior (responsible for the care of creation) from 1981-1983 was notorious in linking his dispensational Christian theology with the conviction that creation would be destroyed when Jesus returned. Until then, creation exists for people to occupy, use and consume (*Washington Post*, May 24, 1981). This argument is developed Calvin Beisner, *Prosperity and Poverty: The Compassionate Use of the Earth's Resources in a World of Scarcity.* (Wifp and Stock, 1988).

- God is Lord of all things, and in fact, all things belong to God.
- People exist in the image of God with a threefold purpose of worshipping God, nourishing relationships with one another, and working to guard creation and help it be fruitful.

Yet Genesis also includes the story of the Fall. Though God created

God did not give the "creation mandate" of Genesis 1-3 without also giving the "economic plan" for how to fulfill it.

in abundance, as Walter Brueggemann says, "We never feel that we have enough; we have to have more and more, and this insatiable desire destroys us. Whether we are liberal or conservative Christians, we must confess that the central problem of our lives is that we are torn apart by the conflict between our attraction to the good news of God's abundance and the power of our belief in scarcity—a belief that makes us greedy, mean, and unneighborly. We spend our lives trying to sort out that ambiguity."[35]

While driving on the freeway the other day, I passed a tanker truck owned by Praxair, and was struck by their corporate tag line, printed in 2 foot tall letters across the tanker: "Making the Planet More Productive." I was struck by their grand vision. They're not just distributing various industrial gases. They are enabling the planet's productivity. They definitely understand the "fruitful" dimension of the creation mandate. Intrigued, when I got home I researched the company. They have carefully developed policies on only marketing conflict free materials, ensuring human rights and guarding against human trafficking, and insisting on practices that ensure sustainable development and mitigate climate change. It was encouraging to read of a company that gets not only the "fruitfulness mandate," but the mandate to guard both the natural creation and human life.[36]

---

[35] Brueggemann, *op cit.*
[36] www.praxair.com.

Just as God gave business-related commands in the beginning—to guard, order, and make fruitful the rest of creation—so God outlined in the rest of the Hebrew Bible an economic system to follow in order to achieve this.

2. The Two Foundations of Biblical Stewardship

Biblical economics is centered in two strong convictions that are to shape our entire approach to money, work, and business.

a. We own nothing. If we are to take the Bible seriously, we are confronted with the assertion that there really is no such thing as private ownership of property. We are stewards, literally caretakers, of someone else's resources. *"The earth is the Lord's and all that is in it"* (Ps. 24:1). *"The land is mine,"* declares the Lord (Lev. 25:23). This radical notion is contrary to nearly every culture's understanding of ownership, especially modern cultures. (Unless, of course, we speak of those cultures where a king, queen or tribe own all the land and others may be granted rights to use it.)

Obviously, this view isn't affirmed by all who read Scripture. Calvin Beisner asserts, "The Bible assigns to the owner of property *absolute control* over it within the limits of moral law (Acts 5.4; Mt 20:13,15)."[37] It strikes me that "absolute control" is rather severely limited by the biblical claim that God owns all property, and our stewardship of it must be for the good of all.

God owns all things and entrusts them to us for our stewardship and use. Jesus stresses in his parables how we are to live and work as stewards of God's resources. Jesus emphasizes over and over this theme of stewardship through parables about vineyards, property managers, the debtor, and landlords he underscores fruitfulness,

---

[37] E. Calvin Beisner, "Managing the Resources of the Earth," in *Readings in Christian Ethics. Vol. 2: Issues and Applications,* ed. David Clark and Robert Rakestraw (Baker, 1996), 387-88. Italics his.

gratitude to God, and the well being of those who are poor as the outcomes of our stewardship. Thirty-eight out of 45 of Jesus' parables occurred in and related to "marketplace" themes. 112 out of 122 public appearances were in the marketplace rather than the Temple. [38] We risk misunderstanding the full implications of Jesus' teaching about money, work, possessions, and stewardship if we "over-spiritualize" these parables, assuming they really refer only to our personal, private relationship with God. Yes, they speak to our relationship with God, but in the context of our relationship with people, and our stewardship of creation.

b. We are all guest workers. God may entrust creation to our care, but nonetheless we are merely tenants. Leviticus 25:23 proclaims, *"The land is mine; with me you are but aliens and tenants."* In the allocation of labor, we are all guest workers, foreign or migrant laborers, so to speak. We work at the invitation of God. This clarifies two things for us:

> **First**, *We recognize our status as servants.* No one dare become too conceited or for that matter, too humiliated about his or her own worth based on quantity of possessions.
> **Second**, *We recognize our dignity.* We are *God's* tenant workers. We don't just work for human bosses or employers; we work for God. "*Render service with enthusiasm, as to the Lord, and not to men and women*" (Eph. 6:6).

Everything hinges on these two foundations. There is a rich freedom in knowing that a God who is faithful and trustworthy owns our possessions. Bondage and conflicted allegiances are likely to arise if we don't recognize this fact.

3. The Biblical Concern About Money
Currency is a social construct. Its value economically hinges on consensus and trust. The 2015 debates in Europe about a common

---

[38] Paul Stevens, *Work Matters: Lessons from Scripture* (Eerdmans, 2012), 134.

currency highlight the fragility of common agreement about the value and nature of money. However, the Bible doesn't regard money as spiritually neutral. [39]

Scripture is filled with warnings that money has a form of emotional and indeed spiritual power. It's not just paper and metal. Rather, it is charged with power. For example, Jesus warns: *"Do not lay up for yourselves treasures on earth"* (Matt. 6:19). *"Woe to you that are rich"* (Luke 6:24). *"You cannot serve God and mammon"* (Luke 16:13). Brueggemann notes, "Jesus said it succinctly …You cannot serve God and do what you please with your money or your sex or your land. And then he says, 'Don't be anxious, because everything you need will be given to you.'" [40]

God owns all things. We are God's stewards. Unless God possesses our possessions, our possessions will possess us.

Yet, the biblical news about money isn't all negative. Jesus frequently uses parables of abundance and prosperity (see for example Matt. 25:14-30; Luke 16). He ate comfortably with those who were rich (Luke 11:37; 14:1). He provided wine for a lavish wedding (John 2:1). Wealthy women supported Jesus and the disciples in their ministry (Luke 8:2-3).

Other than the kingdom of God, Jesus spoke more about money and possessions than any single topic. Because money and possessions possess such power, and can exert power over our souls, we need boundaries and safeguards to protect us from being possessed by it.

Eric Law, founder of the Kaleidoscope Institute for sustainable communities, develops an application of biblical economics for non-

---

[39] For an excellent discussion of this see Richard Foster, *Money, Sex and Power* (Hodder and Stoughton, 1985), 19-87; and Jacques Ellul, *Money and Power* (InterVarsity Press, 1984).

[40] Brueggemann, *op cit.*

cash transactions in his book, *Holy Currencies*. In addition to money, he describes relationships, truth, wellness, leadership, time, and place as currencies. He gives the entire system the intriguing name of *GracEconomics*. "Money is not the only currency we use to value what we need or what we offer. GracEconomics unclutches money's hold on us and invites people to recapture the valuing process using other currencies that have been around long before money was invented."[41] The goal is to honor the dignity and contribution of those who lack financial resources. Though this approach has significant implications, especially for not-for-profit organizations, for the purpose of our study we will focus on business transactions that depend on money.

4. The Costs of Disobedience, the Rewards of Trust

The Hebrew Bible portrays a continuum of outcomes from our economic choices:

At various times in our life, we are likely to be at varying places on this continuum. When individuals and society ignore the two foundational convictions of biblical economics—God owns everything and we are stewards and guest workers—the result is that some people move toward exploitation and bondage. Israel was not simply called to leave the *land* of Egypt, but to leave the *ways* of Egypt. The Bible identifies ancient Egypt not simply as a geographic place but as a way of life, representing the consequences of fallen

[41] Eric H.F. Law, *Holy Currencies* (Chalice Press, 2013). More information can be found at www.kscopeinstitute.org. Soul Kitchen, in Red Bank, New Jersey, is an example of a business that seeks to implement non-cash forms of payment for meals. See www.jbjsoulkitchen.org, and an article in the *Huffington Post* by Wayne Parry, "Soul Kitchen" (Oct 20, 2011).

human life. The economics of oppression stand in sharp contrast to the economics of the kingdom of God:

Economics of the Kingdom of God	Economics of Oppression
Trust	Distrust
Community	Exploitation
Abundance	Scarcity (at least for some)
Harmony	Violence
Justice	Oppression
Equity	Disparity

Once delivered from Pharaoh, a different way of doing business was required if Israel was to stay free in the Promised Land. To prepare Israel for this, while still in the desert between Egypt and Palestine, God outlined an economic system that would keep people out of bondage and ensure the flourishing of all in the Land of Promise.

Later, when prophets were compelled to condemn Israel because it had become too much like ancient Egypt, God judged Israel for failing to trust God with their possessions and for their oppression of the poor. See for example Amos 4:1, Zechariah 7:10, Psalm 49:6, and Proverbs 11:28. Rather than being sent back to Egypt, Israel was sent into captivity in Babylon. We'll explore this more fully later. So possibly our continuum could be changed in this way:

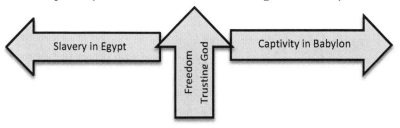

One of the deep roots of our global economic woes is distrust in God. From that springs forth other weeds that choke flourishing and well-being. Because of our distrust in God for our finances and business, we are tempted to think that our economic well-being depends on us: our own effort, control, and defenses. Out of anxiety, we grasp and grab, and are tempted to exploit other people and all of creation to secure our survival and success. As we'll see, the remedy God prescribes is multifaceted: the establishment of systems and practices to nourish trust, promote initiative, and protect creation and people from others' exploitation.

STEWARDSHIP OF TIME AND MONEY

The economic system developed in the Bible is centered in trust in God who owns all things, who honors all people as guest workers in God's kingdom, and who commissions everyone to be stewards of people, time, and God's creation. God's plan is for economic activity to promote the common good—the flourishing of all of God's creation. Individual initiative and responsibility are encouraged and rewarded, while the well-being of those who can't compete is protected because God is committed to the well-being of everyone. This requires boundaries.

The free market regulators on business activity—personal choice, the laws of supply and demand, and market forces—aren't sufficient to ensure the guarding of creation and the well-being of all people. My assertion is that the Hebrew Bible describes another set of regulators—boundaries—according to which the community must abide. Ideally, these are community-owned commitments. But if the community won't abide by them, God will enforce them. We see in the history of Israel the extreme measures to which God went due to their refusal to honor biblical economic commitments.

There is a strong biblical case for the community, both through collective commitment and through government regulations, to erect boundaries around business to ensure that businesses abide by the economic system God has set forth. Of course, many dispute this assertion that business, and indeed the economic system, need community-created boundaries. Some Christian theologians and economists believe that unregulated free markets are the most "Christian" economic system.[42] The Hebrew economy didn't rely on

---

[42] For a fascinating exploration of how free market capitalism came to be identified with Christian faith, see Kevin Kruse, *One Nation Under*

cash (financial capital). However, since land is "capital" in an agrarian economy, I propose that there are several clear principles outlined in the Old Testament and that they are still valid today.

This economic system serves to 1) nourish trust in God; 2) create opportunities and incentives for creative stewardship; and 3) guard the sacredness of people, time, resources, and the name and glory of God that surround us in business (and all of life).

1.   Stewarding Time
Sabbath and Sabbath Year. Beginning with Sabbath rest each week, everyone—rich and poor, human and animals—got a day off from work. The land, environment, and animals were protected from exploitation and destruction (Lev. 25:1-7; 26:34-35). From the opening of Genesis 1 to the Prophetic writings, the Old Testament is filled with almost 100 commands to keep Sabbath. Isaiah utters it as a lament, "refrain from trampling the Sabbath and pursuing your own interests" (Is. 58:13).

Contrast this with our current 24/7 business life, with people having to work three part-time minimum wage jobs in order to provide for their family, and with the impact on animals of maritime feed lots where freighters feed animals during **The Sabbath structures** their international voyage so that they are **our time for trust.** ready for slaughter immediately upon reaching port. In God's eyes, we are not mere workers. All people

---

God: How Corporate America Invented Christian America (Basic Books, 2015). See also his article "How Business made us Christian," *New York Times Sunday Review* (March 15, 2015). For a defence of unregulated, free market capitalism, see Scott Rae, "Made for Responsibility" in *The Pastor's Guide to Fruitful Work and Economic Wisdom,* edited by Drew Cleveland and Greg Forster (Made to Flourish, 2014), 98-108. This is developed in more detail in Austin Hill and Scott Rae, *The Virtues of Capitalism: The Moral Case for Free Markets* (Chicago: Northfield Publishing, 2010).

deserve a day to rest and be restored, for relationships and recreation.

God mandated good physical and environmental stewardship. God's commands became very specific. Trees were not to be destroyed as acts of war (Deut. 20.19). People were to build latrines to ensure sanitation and protect the environment from pollution (Deut. 23.13-14). The Sabbath was not only for people. Fields were to get a Sabbath rest (even a sabbatical). This was to culminate every seven years in a Sabbath year. During this year, the fields would lie fallow. The land would get its rest.

The Sabbath is not just an inhibiting restriction. It is a boundary placed on time for our protection, and for the protection of creation. We are not merely workers. We are created in God's image for joy-filled relationships and for worship. Thus everyone, rich or poor, was to get a day off each week. Not to take a day off, or to permit others to do so, is rooted in distrust in God. We may feel like we need every minute, every gram of labor we can squeeze out of people to accomplish the tasks before us. We may be convinced that if we stop, we'll fall behind. Others will get ahead. We won't have enough. The Sabbath protects us from the idolatry of own effort, the reliance only upon ourselves. God will provide enough.

2. Stewarding Money

Tithing. The human tendency to worship the creation rather than the Creator and to place our trust in the works of our own hands rather than the One who created our hands and empowers our work is well documented.

Tithing structures our money for trust

Pope Benedict described idolatry as "an all-too-common occupational hazard of business life." It emerges when "the sole criterion for action in business is thought to be the maximization of profit; when technology is pursued for its own sake; when personal wealth or political influence fail to serve the common good; or when utilitarian or consequential reasoning becomes dominant."[43]

The biblical laws of tithing provide a safeguard against the idolatry of money. Just as most people feel like they don't have enough time to afford a day off, most people feel like they can't "afford" to give away 10 percent of their income. In doing exactly that, we remind ourselves not only that God is the source of what we have but also that God can be trusted to provide what we need. The Sabbath and tithing help to protect us from the idolatry of our own effort, and re-center our lives in trust of God.

Furthermore, we are commanded to tithe so that *"the stranger, the orphan, and the widow shall eat and be satisfied, so that the Lord your God will bless you in all the enterprises you undertake"* (Deut. 14.22, 29). The commands to keep Sabbath and to tithe are God-given encouragement of trust, and a God-given protection of the rest of creation from human exploitation.

For Reflection and Discussion

What do you think of this possible implication of Sabbath and tithing for contemporary business?

How do you respond to the assertion that a day off for all workers each week, and tithing of our income aren't optional social practices. They are vital protections for our well-being and the well-being of all creation? How do you deal with the question of how realistic this is?

---

[43] Pope Benedict XVI, Encyclical Letter *Caritas in Veritate* (2009), 71; cited in *Vocation of the Business Leader*, 6.

Personal Strategies for Catalyzing Change. What do I believe God is calling me to do within my sphere of responsibilities to steward time and money more wisely?

	Strategies for catalyzing change
Interests: What particularly interests me in terms of business as stewardship?	
Sphere of responsibility: To what extent does my stewardship of time and money align with God's purposes?	
Ways to model the change I value: What can I do immediately?	
Concerns outside my responsibility: What issues and opportunities are outside my role?	
Key people: How can I build key relationships to encourage and support others in their spheres of responsibility (in areas about which I'm concerned)?	
Prayer: For what can I pray?	

If you want to evaluate this and strategize your response further, see *Evaluating How My Business and Work Participate in God's Purposes*

4. Stewardship of Work and Wages

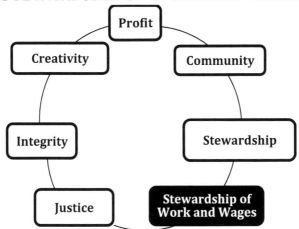

This section continues the exploration of the biblical economic system, focusing specifically on its implications for employment, income inequality, provision for those who can't work, and treatment of foreign workers.

By the end, participants should be able to draw connections to ancient biblical teaching and pressing issues in our contemporary society regarding work and wages.

CENTRAL QUESTIONS: What the relevance of economic principles for an agrarian, cashless society, and our contemporary financial life? What does the Bible say about how we should provide for the unemployed and for immigrant workers?

ENSURE ACCESS TO GOOD WORK

As we've seen, God mandated work. We are to enable and protect the fruitfulness of God's creation. Work is intended to be a good expression of our creative life in the image of the Creator (working) God. The Old Testament outlines an economic system that honors individual responsibility, and encourages wealth generation and productivity, while at the same time protects those who can't compete, and protects future generations from being perpetually penalized (or unfairly profiting) from their parents labor. Protections for the poor, and for those who couldn't compete in the economic system were created through the laws of gleaning, restraints placed on debt and indentured servitude, and restrictions on the ancient (and likewise very modern) practice of exorbitant interest rates.

1. Honor Individual Responsibility

The economic system that God ordained in the Old Testament affirms individual initiative and responsibility, and the freedom to acquire wealth (Lev. 27; Deut. 24:10-13). All who are able must fulfill their responsibility for their livelihood (Lev. 25:25-43; Deut. 15:12-14). Scripture abounds with exhortations to work, invitations to enjoy the fruit of one's labor, and warnings about laziness (Prov. 6:6-11; 14:23; 23:21; 24:30-34). Fruitful work is part of God's good creation. Those who showed initiative were free to amass wealth, acquire property, and enjoy prosperity. There has been a theme throughout history that prosperity is a reward for faithful work and a sign of God's blessing. Conversely, poverty is viewed as the consequence of laziness and a sign of judgment.[44]

---

[44] Certainly the classic study on the relationship of faith in God, hard work, and prosperity is Max Weber's, *The Protestant Ethic and the Spirit of Capitalism*, trans. by Talcott Parsons (New York: Scribners, 1958).

However, as we'll see later, Scripture is also clear that amassing wealth without regard for the well-being of others places one on the path of judgment.

The controversy in recent years over the income disparity between Chief Executives and other workers highlights this question. In the 1940s, CEOs earned on average 20 times the salary of average workers. In 2010, Fortune 500 company CEOS earned 325 times the income of average workers in their companies.[45] The news networks "lit up" in 2015 with reports about the extraordinary minimum wage one business owner inaugurated for his staff. Dan Price, founder and owner of Gravity Payments in Seattle, surprised all who heard when he announced to his employees that he was reducing his CEO salary from $1 million to the new minimum wage for his employees of $70,000 a year. When he studied at Seattle Pacific University, the tagline for their School of Business and Economics was "Another way of doing business." Dan took this to heart. Something other than the laws of supply and demand should shape his business that had a net profit of over $2 million in 2014. "The market rate for me as a C.E.O. compared to a regular person is ridiculous, it's absurd," he commented. "As much as I'm a capitalist, there is nothing in the market that is making me do it." Rather, he wanted his staff to earn enough to buy a house, pay for their children's education, and have a reasonable quality of life.[46]

---

[45] To view this graphically, see http://billmoyers.com/2015/01/05/top-10-charts-2014; and http://www.npr.org/sections/money/2014/10/02/349863761/40-years-of-income-inequality-in-america-in-graphs.

[46] "One Company's New Minimum Wage: $70,000 a Year," *New York Times*, April 13, 2015. His action provoked admiration and opposition, gained new customers and lost others. It won the hearts of some employees while others quit because this seemed unfair. See "A company copes with backlash against the raise that roared." *New York Times Business Day.* July 31, 2015.

2.   Ensure equal opportunity every generation: jubilee

Because our place of birth has such a determinative impact on our quality and way of life—and because no one chooses this—Scripture outlines a strategy to "level the playing field" and give everyone equal opportunity. First of all, every seven years was to be a Sabbath year. All of creation was to get a sabbatical (not just academics). The fertility of the land would be restored through a year of rest. Then, every seven cycles of Sabbath years (50 years) was to be the Jubilee. In this year, all debts would be forgiven and all slaves would be freed. Neither debt nor indentured labor could permanently trap people in poverty. Furthermore, all land would be returned to its original division among the 12 Tribes.

The purpose of this law was to protect people from structural disadvantages that kept some perpetually poor. Every generation all families received a fresh start and equal access to the means of production and wealth generation. In an agrarian economy, "economic capital" is land (Deut. 15:1-6, 12-17; Lev. 25). Individual initiative (or lack of initiative), and private property were honored—but within boundaries that prevented multigenerational wealth accumulation among an elite, and perpetual impoverishment among those on the margins.

The right to private property receives limited affirmation in the biblical economic system. It is accepted, but only when property is stewarded for the common good. Pope Francis stressed this in his encyclical *Laudato Si'*: "The Christian tradition has never recognized the right to private property as absolute or inviolable, and has stressed the social purpose of all forms of private property." He quotes Pope John Paul II's statement, "the Church does indeed defend the legitimate right to private property, but she also teaches no less clearly that there is always a social mortgage on all private property, in order that the goods may serve the general purpose that God gave them."[47]

Multi-generational transfer of wealth or poverty was limited (Lev 25:1-17, 23-24). Although the fruits of one's labor could be inherited (personal possessions and livestock), the means of wealth generation (land) was to be equally divided once every 50 years. Those who were entrepreneurial could immediately set to work expanding their prosperity. Those who were slothful could sell themselves back into slavery the next day. Regardless, once a lifetime everyone could experience a fresh start. This minimized both the "slavery" and the unfair privilege of multi-generational transfer of poverty and wealth. The law of Jubilee made certain that slavery couldn't be perpetuated by ensuring that the children of slaves were not automatically themselves enslaved. Similarly, I propose that one of God's purposes for business is to provide opportunities so that everyone who is able can gain access to the necessary means for generating their own income once in every lifetime.

A special concern for businesses and society is to provide access for those in poverty to employment and to the means of earning a living. This is a contemporary equivalent to the Jubilee call for all land to be equally redistributed once a lifetime. God calls all societies to ensure that those in poverty have access to employment. Much of the contemporary discussion of economic growth focuses on the need to develop and strengthen the "middle class" whose purchases are the engine that drives economic growth. As influential as those on the top or at the middle of an economic system may be,

---

[47] Francis, *Laudato Si': On Care for Our Common Home* (2015), 93: 69.; citing John Paul II, *Address to Indigenous and Rural People*, Cuilapan, Mexico (29 January 1979), 6: *AAS* 72 (1070), 209.

it's inescapably evident that Scripture calls for a resolute commitment to those who are on the bottom of the economy.[48]

For Reflection and Discussion

What do you think of this possible implication of Jubilee for contemporary business? *Special care must be exercised to give all people access during their lifetime to the means required to provide for their own livelihood and well being. It is worth exploring whether inheritance laws (taxes) that limit the multi-generational family transfer of wealth are integral to the common good and everyone's well-being.[49]*

3. Protect those who can't compete: gleaning

The law of gleaning provides an agrarian example that has implications for cash economies. *"You shall not strip your vineyard bare, or gather the fallen grapes of your vineyard; you shall leave them for the poor and the alien"* (Leviticus 19:10). Because the biblical economic system is oriented towards ensuring the well-being of all people, and not just enhancing some people's prosperity, laws were established as foundational commitments to protect those who are outside the economic system and can't compete—the poor, widows, orphans, elderly, and aliens. Leaving some of the harvest for those who are without access to employment is a way to ensure they have food, while at the same time honoring their dignity and sense of responsibility. Rather than a handout, they, too, have the opportunity to work for their livelihood. This does not imply that those in poverty are condemned not only to working three minimum wage jobs to support their family, plus go to the food bank to "glean." Rather, it raises the concern about how society

---

[48] For an interesting analysis of this, and development of the implications, see Warren R. Copeland, *And the Poor Get Welfare: The Ethics of Poverty in the United States* (Nashville : Abingdon Press in cooperation with the Churches' Center for Theology and Public Policy, Washington, D.C., 1994).

[49] For action in this regard among the world's billionaires, see http://givingpledge.org.

structures itself to ensure that those who can't compete successfully (or even sufficiently) in the marketplace, gain enough resources to sustain themselves in ways that honor both their dignity and responsibility.

The US Department of Agriculture has picked up on the contemporary relevance of this ancient practice. 100 billion pounds of food are thrown away each year in the US (20% of the entire food supply), yet 49 million Americans are undernourished and food insecure. In response, the USDA is encouraging modern day gleaning, "Gleaning is simply the act of collecting excess fresh foods from farms, gardens, farmer's markets, grocers, restaurants, state/county fairs, or any other sources in order to provide it to those in need."[50]

Those who can't compete because of age, sex, or infirmity are to be protected and provided for (see among many passages Lev. 23:22; Deut. 24:17-22). Throughout the Bible we find continual affirmation of God's special concern for the poor. Hannah proclaims at the birth of Samuel, *"The Lord raises up the poor from the dust and lifts the needy from the ash heap, to make them sit with princes and inherit a seat of honor"* (1 Sam. 2:8). Ecclesiastes proclaims that God sees the *"tears of the oppressed"* (Eccles. 4:1). In fact, Ezekiel proclaims that the sin of Sodom wasn't only sexual immorality (as has often been suggested) but also hardness of heart toward those who were poor. Sodom had *"plenty of bread, and untroubled tranquility; yet she did not strengthen the hand of the poor and the needy"* (Ezek. 16.49).

In the biblical economic system ensures the well being of non-competitive people. Instead of being oriented only around the "social insiders" and those with wealth and the means to buy their goods and services, businesses (and all of society) are to have a

---

[50] *"Let's Glean: USDA Gleaning Toolkit,"* www.usda.gov/documenets/usda_gleaning_toolkit.pdf.

special concern for people who can't compete and are outsiders. We are to guard the dignity of those in poverty, by ensuring they have means to provide for themselves and their families. Job-training initiatives, affirmative hiring practices and even micro-loans may be a contemporary equivalent to gleaning the leftover crops. Rather than simply giving those who are unemployed gifts of food and commodities—which is an essential relief activity during times of crisis—the call is also to create access to the employment that is necessary for them to help themselves.

For Reflection and Discussion
What do you think of this possible implication of the law of gleaning for contemporary business? *Special care and provision must be extended for those who are not yet able to be significant producers or consumers. Creating employment opportunities for those who are often excluded from access to work is central to God's purposes for business.*

4. Honor Foreign Workers
God's mandate for business development begins from the opposite end of society than is expected in most cultures. Rather than placing the primary focus on how to manage and invest wealth, God focuses on those in poverty. Rather than beginning with the affluent, God begins by addressing our responsibility to empower and guard the dignity of those who are vulnerable.

In the biblical economy, the rights of foreign workers and immigrants are protected (Lev. 25.47-55; Deut. 24.14-15, 17). Repeatedly in the Hebrew Bible, Israel was reminded that they too are guest workers on God's land. *"You shall not oppress a stranger; you know the feelings of the stranger, for you were strangers in the land of Egypt"* (Exodus 23.9; see also Deut. 10.19; Jer. 22.3). They, too, were once aliens, foreign workers, exploited laborers. Therefore, they must continually exercise special concern for the rights and well being of aliens in their midst. *"When a stranger dwells among you, you are not to maltreat him…you shall love him like yourself"* (Leviticus 19.34).

For Reflection and Discussion

In the midst of our contemporary crisis over foreign labor—migrant workers, guest workers, economic refugees, undocumented laborers and immigrants—what do you think of this possible implication of the laws for treatment of foreign workers for contemporary business?

What are the implications in the debate about the rights of citizens vs. non-citizens when we view the debate through our common identity as God's guest laborers, resident aliens, and people who are invited by God to steward God's land and resources?

CONTRIBUTE TO TRUSTWORTHINESS IN SOCIETY

God is deeply concerned about trust. God's steadfast, trustworthy love and faithfulness are portrayed in Scripture as integral to God's nature. As creatures in the image of God, our ability to trust God and live trustworthy lives is central to flourishing. Business has a central purpose in this since it deals with life at very vulnerable points. (We will examine this more fully in a subsequent section.)

1. Wages and working conditions

Businesses build trust by paying workers the wage they are due (Lev. 19.13; Deut. 15.13-14); by not cheating workers (Deut. 24.14-15); and by making sure people having to work away from home get time off to return to their families (1 Kings 5.28).

It is often overlooked that an integral aspect of the US Civil Rights movement was addressing not just racism, but lack of access to jobs that paid a livable wage. Martin Luther King, Jr. asserted that all people had the right to guaranteed employment (and for those who couldn't work), guaranteed income at a "living wage."[51]

---

[51] See Michael Greene, *A Way Out of No Way: The Economic Prerequisites of the Beloved Community* (Eugene, Oregon: Cascade Books, 2014).

2. Honest contracts

Business has the purpose of ensuring trustworthiness in the fabric of society by leading the way in ensuring the just settlement of disputes and guaranteeing faithfulness to contracts (Deut. 16:18-20). Anti-bribery laws aren't recent inventions (see Exod. 23.8). To make false contracts and to tell lies is a form of theft (Lev. 19.11). God mandated fair wages, honest trade, and accurate scales and prices in the marketplace as consequences of sincere worship (Lev. 19.35-36; Micah 6:10-12). A false scale is an abomination to God (Proverbs 11.1).

WHAT IF BUSINESSES FAIL TO ABIDE BY THESE BOUNDARIES?

There is little historical evidence that Israel practiced the economic system outlined in the Levitical code except for weekly Sabbath observances, tithing, and the prohibition of usury. It's unlikely that the Sabbath year, Jubilee, the release of slaves, forgiveness of debts, and return of the land to the original distribution among the 12 Tribes were ever implemented.

The biblical scholar John Howard Yoder documents that by the time of Jesus, an elaborate system called *prosboul* had been created, through which debts could be given to the courts just before the Sabbath year—and returned intact to the debt owners immediately afterwards. That way debt could be retained. "This was in the form of an act of *prosboul*, the text of which has been preserved in the Mishnah: *'I _____ transmit to you _____, judges at _____ my credit, in order to be able to recover whatever sum is due to me from _____whatever might be the date when I express desire.'"*[52]

The consequences of not living with business practices that are founded in trust in God lead to captivity in Babylon. Leviticus warns

---

[52] John Howard Yoder, *The Politics of Jesus* (Eerdmans, 1994), 65.

that the land will lie desolate for every year Israel failed to give it Sabbath rest (Lev. 26:43). Jeremiah proclaimed the fulfillment of this in Israel's captivity for 70 years in Babylon—the consequence of almost five centuries without a Sabbath Year (Jeremiah 25:11; 29:10. See also 2 Chronicles 36:20-21). However, God was committed to all of creation, and not just to humans. Therefore, whether by the preferred response of Israel's obedient choice, or by God's forceful intervention, the land would get its Sabbath.

The economic hope for the Messiah. The belief that God would send a deliverer, a Messiah, to free Israel from oppressors, and provide for those who were vulnerable and in poverty became a strong part of Israel's hope. This is profoundly expressed in the Magnificat of Mary: *"He has brought down the powerful and lifted up the lowly; he has filled the hungry with good things, and sent the rich away empty"* (Luke 1:52–53).

Most cultures interpret prosperity as a sign of blessing and poverty as a sign of abandonment.[53] In Jesus' first sermon, as recorded in Luke 4, he proclaims God's great social reversal and the inauguration of God's ordained economic system. Quoting Isaiah 61, he declares, *"The Spirit of the Lord is upon me, because the Lord has anointed me; he has sent me to bring good news to the poor...to proclaim the year of the Lord's favor."*

This is repeated in his Sermon on the Mount when he proclaims that it is the poor and the hungry, the meek and the marginalized that are blessed (Matt. 5). The "year of the Lord's favor" was understood by Jews to announce the inauguration of the Jubilee. Jesus went on in his first sermon to say that it was foreigners who were most commendable for their faithfulness to God's laws. It is

---

[53] For a series of articles that concisely evaluate the "Prosperity Gospel," see *Christianity Today*, July 12, 2007. Online at www.christianitytoday.com/ct/2007/july/12.html.

no wonder that his hearers actually tried to kill him after this first sermon. Jesus was proclaiming the Year of Jubilee for all people and held up "outsiders" as models of faith (Luke 4:29). He was directly challenging the established economic and social order.

The following chart summarizes these themes that shape the biblical economic system:

The Principles of Biblical Economics		
God Owns All Things		We Are Stewards
Safeguards for Stewardship: To encourage fruitful stewardship, to protect us from idolatry of our own effort and resources, and to guard the sacredness of people, time, and creation God establishes boundaries		
Boundary on Time: Sabbath		Boundary on Money: Tithing
Boundaries on Work and Wages:		
Protect Creation The land, environment, and animals are protected from exploitation and destruction (Lev. 25:1-7; 26:34-35)	**Private Property** Private property and individual initiative are protected and honored (Lev. 27; Dt. 24:10-13)	**Inheritance** The multi-generational transfer and inheritance of extreme poverty and wealth are prohibited (Lev. 25:1-17, 23-24)
Opportunity All people are to have equal access once a lifetime to the means of production and wealth generation (Deut. 15:1-6, 12-17; Lev. 25)	**Responsibility** Individual responsibility for our livelihood and stewardship is mandated (Lev. 25:25-43; Deut. 15:12-14)	**Protection** Those who can't compete because of age, gender, or infirmity are protected and provided for (Lev. 23:22; Dt. 24:17-22)
Foreign labor The rights of foreign workers and immigrants are protected (Lev. 25.47-55; Dt. 24.14-17)	**Wages** Fair wages, trade and markets are required (Micah 6:10-12)	**Contracts** Just settlement of disputes and faithfulness to contracts are guaranteed (Dt. 16:18-20)

For Reflection and Discussion

1. What's your reaction to this overview of a biblical economic system?

2. What is your reaction to this glance into this boundaried economic system? On a scale of 1 to 5, with 1 being irrelevant and 5 being exactly what our business environment needs, where would you rank this? Why?

Protection of all people from idolatry

1	2	3	4	5
irrelevant	impractical	nice theory	intriguing	vital

Protection of creation (land, natural resources, plants/animals)

1	2	3	4	5
irrelevant	impractical	nice theory	intriguing	vital

Protection of those who can't compete or provide for selves

1	2	3	4	5
irrelevant	impractical	nice theory	intriguing	vital

Protection of individual initiative, responsibility and dignity

1	2	3	4	5
irrelevant	impractical	nice theory	intriguing	vital

3. How do you respond to the objections that these boundaries would reduce incentive, hinder the flexibility of a business to adapt to changes in its marketplace, increase costs of operation and make a business uncompetitive. After all, customers and clients will go to the lowest cost supplier.

CORPORATE SOCIAL RESPONSIBILITY

Those with financial resources have as much a need to share them as those without have the need to receive. The need to give and receive goes both directions. Charitable giving isn't merely an optional expression of kindness or benevolence. Since, in American law, corporations have the same rights and legal status as persons, I propose that they have the same mandate as individuals to use some of their profits for the common good. Though businesses aren't charities, they share the same commitments to social responsibility as all "persons." We see this expressed in corporations adopted social responsibility codes of conduct, charitable funds, and foundations. Even government taxation can be a form of profit sharing to benefit the common good.[54]

Though it is very commendable when businesses give away a portion of their profits to charitable causes, we've asserted that the social responsibility of a business includes far more than what it does with its profits. All the bottom lines of business contribute to a business's fulfillment of its corporate responsibility. The concerns of business extend to what occurs in the lives of all stakeholders—employees, customers, suppliers, those indirectly impacted by the business, and the natural environment. We are called to ask, what happens to their dignity, character, community, hopes, and dreams as a result of our business? This is the topic of our next section.

For Reflection and Discussion

What's your response to the following assertion? *If corporations want to be treated legally with the same rights and protections as other "persons," then they share the same biblical responsibility as all persons to exercise special care to steward their wealth for the common good, and even to give a portion of their profits to care for others.*

Of course whether a business fulfills these purposes is beyond the scope of individual workers. These are macro-level concerns. However, to live with joy and contentment, knowing that I am indeed participating in a holy calling, it is vital that each of us can see connections between the purposes we are serving in our

---

[54] For more on this, see the Foundation for Corporate Social Responsibility. www.fcsr.pl.

workplace and these larger purposes. Every individual within their sphere of authority can contribute to moving closer toward God's purposes within their sphere of responsibility.

The purposes our businesses serve have far-reaching consequences on the quality of our own and others' character, and on the fabric of communities.

Sometimes we may have to assess whether it's possible to align our particular business with the purposes of God. If we can't change the purposes of our business to align with the purposes of God, we risk having our business change us in ways that are contrary to God's will. To put this danger in extreme terms, we risk building our economy and lives, and even trying to worship God, upon contemporary equivalents to the Goree Island slave fort.

In extreme situations, changing employers may be the only option.

We may succeed in increasing people's affluence and improve people's quality of life by satisfying their needs for goods and services—but actually impoverish people in their deeper needs and values.

It is possible to increase financial wealth yet deepen other forms of poverty.

- Does our business encourage individualism that produces competitiveness and selfishness? *People may become richer in commodities, but poorer in community.*
- Does our business encourage materialism that produces greed and envy? *People may become richer in what they consume, but poorer in their character.*
- Does our business encourage secularism that produces reliance on our own effort and things? *People can be richer in material substance, but poorer in spiritual depth.*

- Does our business encourage hedonism and competition that undermine morality and community? *People may become richer in economic value, but poorer in personal values.*

Personal Strategies for Catalyzing Change. What do I think God is calling me to do within my sphere of responsibilities to contribute to meaningful work and fare wages?

	Strategies for catalyzing change
Interests: Of aspect of biblical teaching regarding the stewardship of work and wages most interests me?	
Sphere of responsibility: How can my role contribute to addressing this?	
Ways to model the change I value: What can I do immediately?	
Concerns outside my responsibility: What issues and opportunities are outside my role?	
Key people: How can I build key relationships to encourage and support others in their spheres of responsibility (in areas about which I'm concerned)?	
Prayer: For what can I pray?	

If you want to evaluate this and strategize your response further, see *Evaluating How My Business and Work Participate in God's Purposes*

5.
JUSTICE: BUSINESS IS CALLED TO CONTRIBUTE TO MAKING LIFE RIGHT

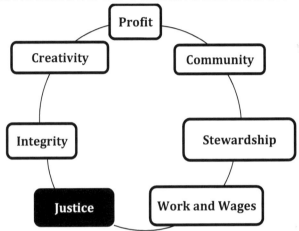

This section examines the role of business in contributing to justice: *life being made right.*

By the end, participants should have an expanded appreciation for ways business can serve God's purpose by contributing to justice in society.

CENTRAL QUESTIONS: What connection do you see between your work and making life right for others (justice)? What's your reaction to the notion that our Sunday prayers need to be matched by our pursuit of economic justice on Monday?

"The Lord has a controversy with his people.... He has told you, O mortal, what is good; and what does the Lord require of you but to do justice, and to love

kindness, and to walk humbly with your God? The voice of the Lord cries to the city...Can I forget the treasures of wickedness in the house of the wicked...Can I tolerate wicked scales and bags of dishonest weights? Your wealthy are full of violence; your inhabitants speak lies. "Micah 6:2, 8–12

CONTRIBUTING TO A FAIR BALANCE

1. Just Business

Justice Defined: Typically we associate "justice" with law: vindicating what's right by punishing wrongdoers and rewarding those who've been treated unfairly. That's true, but I suggest it's too limited. The English word comes from the Latin for righteousness and equity. The same meaning is conveyed in Scripture. For to do justice is to make life right, to establish right order to relationships in society, and to ensure fairness for the good of all.

The will of God is to make life right. If we want our relationship with God to be right—if we want our worship to please God—then

> **The prayers we utter for forgiveness in our sanctuaries *must be matched by* how we further economic justice in the marketplace.**

our financial relationships with others need to be right. Merely deepening our prayer life while we engage in dishonest practices in business, or even practices that destructively consume time and resources, won't draw us closer to God.[55] Intensifying our zeal in worship while we amass fortunes by damaging creation, exploiting people, abusing power, taking advantage of unfair or unjust laws, or ignoring those who are poor won't bring us "credit" before God.

No wonder Micah speaks so strongly regarding the connection between having right order in our business relationships and right order in our relationship with God. Regardless of whether a business is small and simply seeking ways to survive in a competitive

---

[55] Tom Nelson, *Work Matters: Connecting Sunday Worship to Monday Work* (Crossway, 2011).

marketplace, or a transnational corporation that shapes entire economies—*every business has a role in making life right*—doing justice. This can occur through providing meaningful work, ensuring livelihoods that contribute to human flourishing, providing goods and services that enhance human life, and guarding and protecting the natural creation. Every employee, regardless of the extent of their influence in their company, has a role in making life right for others.[56]

For good or for ill, every business has significant impact on life being made right (or not) in the lives of suppliers, customers, workers, and the environment. The historical impact of business on people's well-being is stunning.

In the early 19th century, the average life expectancy globally was 26 years. Today, the World Health Organization estimates it globally to be 70 years.[57]

In 1800, a worker in the Western world labored for an hour to purchase enough oil to light a lamp for 10 minutes. Today, the average Western worker can pay for nearly a year's electricity for one reading light with an hour's work. In 1900, Americans spent

---

[56] For a discussion of business, justice and human rights, see John Ruggie, *Just Business: Multinational Corporations and Human Rights* (Norton, 2013). For justice as it pertains to ethical issues, see Alec Hill's excellent book, *Just Business: Christian Ethics in the Marketplace* (InterVarsity Press, 2008). For a forum on related issues, see the C3Leaders Roundtable at http://www.c3leaders.com/just-business-roundtable.

[57] Angus Maddison, *The World Economy: A Millennial Perspective* (Paris Development Centre of the Organization for Economic Co-operation and Development, 2001), 30; cited in P.J. Hill, "Made for Dignity," in *The Pastor's Guide*, 111.

76% of their income on food, clothing, and housing. In 2010 it was 37%.[58]

For Reflection and Discussion
What's your reaction to this assertion that business has an integral role to making life right?

How does this impact your attitude toward business?

The contribution of business to justice isn't automatic or inevitable. Watch the provocative portrayal of the true costs of the goods we buy at http://storyofstuff.org. What do you think is the relationship between justice and the true cost of products?

An example of the impact of business on justice is clearly evident in the spread of mobile phones. Because of business innovation and customer demand, the cell phone has developed from its origin in 1983 as a $4,000, two-pound machine, to inexpensive devices that in 2015 are accessible to 85% of the world's population. In addition to all the normal communication, relationship, and safety benefits, the spread of mobile phones has contributed to justice and well-being in multiple ways:

- *Access to education:* Entire courses as well as information are now at the fingertips of millions who previously could not dream of attending school. For example, the *Half the Sky* mobile game is teaching women around the world essential business and health skills.[59]
- *Health care:* Phones are reducing response time to critical diseases from the days (or weeks) it takes to transport a patient to hospital, to just a few minutes in which medical professionals can be consulted and assistance gained.

---

[58] Matt Ridley, *The Rational Optimist: How Prosperity Evolves* (New York: Harper, 2010), 34-35; cited in *The Pastor's Guide*, 111.
[59] See www.halftheskymovement.org.

- *Public accountability:* Governments and police are now more accountable through instant broadcasting by text messages, mobile videos.
- *Environmental stewardship:* People in rural areas are able to instantly report illegal logging and poaching.
- *Fair prices:* By being able to check the fair market price for their products, producers can hold middle persons accountable to pay fair prices. All it takes is a simple phone call and everyone can know the real value of his or her product.
- *Improved agriculture:* There is an emerging movement of "telephone farmers." IBM's EZ-Farm project is helping small farmers install water sensors, infrared cameras, and other tools so they can monitor their field and crops from their phones. Not just rain clouds but also the Digital Cloud are assisting agriculture through a web app MbeguChoice. The app helps farmers determine the best seeds, best sources, and best cultivation methods.[60]
- *Stopping corruption:* With the advent of electronic financial transactions on cell phones, many majority world marketplaces are being cleaned up from corruption. Direct electronic payment via cell phones keeps money from being syphoned off and pocketed through bribes and extortion. Rather than simply a tool of entertainment or social networking, cell phones are becoming vital guardians of fair and just marketplaces.[61]
- *Disaster response:* Mobile phones are making it possible to immediately track disasters and coordinate response to ensure the provision of services where they are most needed.

---

[60] Tom Jackson, "Telephone farmers' reaping the benefits of agri-tech," *BBC News,* July 31, 2015.

[61] For an interesting report on the global economic impact of mobile phones, see the study by the A.T. Kearney company, *"The Mobile Economy: 2013,"* www.atkearney.com/documents/10192/70890/The_Mobile_Econo my_2013.pdf.

These are some of the positives for mobile technology. There are also disturbing issues of injustice in their manufacturing and disposal.

- *Conflict minerals:* Some of the metals used in phones and their batteries are mined in conflict areas. In response, US companies must now report the sources of these minerals used in their products, but this doesn't necessarily apply internationally.[62] There are now rankings for companies that produce "conflict-free" products. In 2012, Intel had the best rating; Apple was 9th, Nokia 12th, with LG, Samsung, and Toshiba near the bottom.[63]

- *Working conditions:* Though the report is shrouded by controversy, one of the largest manufacturing companies of phones with almost 1 million employees is Foxconn. It has been subjected to numerous undercover exposés of their highly secretive and controlling labor practices.[64]

- *Electrical power:* Not even considering the electricity required to charge phones, the data storage and routing centers in the "Cloud" on which internet communication depends, consumes the equivalent annual output of 30 nuclear power plants. The diesel generators used to power Silicon Valley's data centers place them on the California government's *Toxic Air Contaminant Inventory.*[65]

- *Toxic waste.* The lead, copper, nickel, and zinc in phones and their batteries are classified as toxic waste. 80% of the US's "e-waste" is exported to majority world countries, such as China, Nigeria, India, Vietnam, and Pakistan, bringing with it cancer-causing dioxins, contaminated air, and undrinkable water. A National Public Radio report described this as a "cyber-age

---

[62] Dodd-Frank Wall Street Reform and Consumer Protection Act, 2010.
[63] See www.raisehopeforcongo.org/content/conflict-minerals-company-rankings.
[64] "The Real Price of an IPhone 5: Life in the Foxconn factory," *The Guardian*, Sept 13, 2102.
[65] "Power, Pollution and the Internet," *New York Times*, Sept. 22, 2012.

nightmare." "Thousands of women on any given day are sitting...basically coking printed circuit boards. As a result, they're breathing all of the brominated flame retardants and the lead and tin that are being heated up." [66]

Once again we return to the touchstone of reality—all of our lives, and obviously all business practices are on a continuum of alignment (or not) with God's purposes. None of us, and therefore no business, is perfect. Honesty is required to admit (and not rationalize) where we are. Grace is required to accept God's love and presence in our current position. And the Spirit is required to propel us forward. As we will see in a subsequent section, the Spirit is the source of creativity, empowering us with dreams, visions, and courage to live more and more closely God's way amidst the upside down realities of our world. As we've already seen, that's also why we need our churches to provide the support, nurture, and challenge for all aspects of our discipleship, and particularly, to live business as a holy calling.

In terms of mobile phones, one creative, right-making response is "green" phones. Similar to the global outcry against "blood, or conflict diamonds," by 2017, it's estimated that 400 million "green phones" will be sold. Standards have been created for sustainable, just impact phones, and as public conviction grows, they will more and more become the norm.[67]

---

[66] Jim Pluckett, "What happens to electronic waste?" NPR Dec 10, 2010. http://www.npr.org/2010/12/21/132204954/after-dump-what-happens-to-electronic-waste. An organization seeking to address this is e-Stewards. See www.e-stewards.org.

[67] See "Behind the Label: The Cell Phone Industry," *Ecosalon,* Oct 3, 2012.

2. Overcoming Economic Sins

Much of the suffering that devastates human life is created by a combination of economic injustice, ethnic prejudice, environmental degradation, and political and personal greed. Undocumented workers risk their lives to sneak into more affluent countries— sometimes escaping war, but sometimes because international trade agreements have wiped out local agriculture and jobs. Pollution and drought have made life unsustainable. Corrupt politicians, gangs, or cartels have made individual economic activity impossible without paying protection money or bribes. These forces overwhelm those on the margins who are without access to power.

We can therefore speak of "economic" sins and not just personal or spiritual sins. As Gustavo Gutiérrez says, "In the Bible, material poverty is a sub-human situation, the fruit of injustice and sin."[68]

Justice isn't a set of "extra" activities tagged onto other business practices. To walk in the way of God, both businesses and individuals will *do justice, love mercy, and walk humbly.* The depth of our love for God is evidenced in our economic activities that ensure justice in the marketplace—fair measures, good wages, truthful transactions, and contribution to the common good. Poverty is provoked both by values and attitudes in the heads and hearts of individuals, as well as by the abuse of power in the marketplace.

---

[68]Gustavo Gutiérrez, *A Theology of Liberation* (1971); see also *Gustavo Gutierrez: Spiritual Writings* (Orbis Books, 2011). For other reflections on this, see Justin Welby, *Can Companies Sin?* (Grove Books, 1992). Alfred Chandler and Bruce Mazlish, editors, *Leviathans: Multinational Corporations and the New Global History* (Cambridge University Press, 2005),

Everyone, whether rich or poor, manager or low-level employee, needs the economic justice of the kingdom.

Everyone needs to be set free from the curses of greed and of desperation in order to thrive in God's kingdom.

Everyone needs to be set free from identities that have been flawed through the ravages of wealth and poverty, and to have our dignity restored as children of God.

Everyone needs the justice that sets us free from the traps of independence and erosive dependence.

This isn't to suggest that all the factors that contribute to justice (or injustice) in society rest in the offices, shop floors, and spreadsheets of business. Business only has one part in this. In a fascinating book on *Why Nations Fail*, the authors assert that:

> "Countries differ in their economic success because of their different institutions, the rules influencing how the economy works, and the incentives that motivate people...Economic institutions must secure private property, an unbiased system of law, and a provision of public services that provide a level playing field in which people can exchange and contract; it also must permit the entry of new businesses and allow people to choose their careers."[69]

Those factors depend upon the broader community, and on governments and civil society. Gary Haugen offers an important analysis of the determinative impact of the rule of law on poverty in his book, *The Locust Effect*.[70] However, ensuring trustworthiness in

---

[69] Daron Acemoglu and James A. Robinson, *Why Nations Fail: The Origins of Power, Prosperity, and Poverty* (New York: Crown Publishers, 2012), 73-75; cited in David Wright, "Made for Community" in *The Pastor's Guide to Fruitful Work and Economic Wisdom*, edited by Drew Cleveland and Greg Forster (Made to Flourish, 2013), 91-92.

[70] Gary Haugen, *The Locust Effect: Why the End of Poverty Requires the End of Violence* (Oxford University Press, 2014).

exchanges, abiding by the rule of law, and insisting on transparency in transactions are directly within the scope of business.

- Businesses don't pay bribes because bribery destroys trust.
- Businesses don't provide ransoms because they create bad businesses.
- Businesses don't give kickbacks because they undermine integrity.
- Businesses protect the environment for its own sake because God made it, for the sake of the poor, and for the sake of the well-being of everyone, including future generations.[71]

Just as we can speak of social justice, we speak of economic justice; among human rights, we can also mention economic rights. We propose that everyone has a right to access to a "living wage."[72] Martin Luther King, Jr. called for the creation of an "economic bill of rights." Speaking of the relationship between work and justice, King said, "When you have mass unemployment in the Negro community, it's called a social problem; when you have mass unemployment in the white community, it's called a depression."[73] King noted that there was 40% unemployment in 1968 among Black youth. Nearly 50 years later, little has changed.

Though sometimes government has a role as the "employer of last resort," businesses are the primary driver for meaningful employment.[74] An example of this is found in Seametrics, a business that makes sophisticated flow meters for water and chemicals.[75] Curt

---

[71] For the relationship between business, the environment and the impact on people in poverty, see Pope Francis' 2015 encyclical, *Laudato Si.*

[72] For a discussion of this, see Richard Horsley, *Covenant Economics: A Biblical Vision of Justice,* (John Knox Press, 2009).

[73] Martin Luther King, Jr. "*Showdown for Nonviolence,*" Look Magazine, Vol 32, April 16, 1968: 23-25.

[74] Michael Green develops this notion from King's thought in *A Way Out of No Way: The Economic Prerequisites of the Beloved Community* (Cascade, 2014).

[75] www.seametrics.com.

is a member of my church and is passionate about this business he founded. By helping farmers manage their use of water, they can protect our global water supply. By helping factories, mines, and sewage facilities treat waste, they help protect the environment. By helping utilities ensure the right amount of chemicals are added to purify drinking water, they can guard people's health.

Curt comments, "What we do in some little way makes the world a better place. We call this technology with a mission, a mission to save time, save money, and to help save the world's resources." He also does this through intentionally locating his factor close to where chronically unemployed populations live (immigrant, ethnic minority), and intentionally hiring from these groups for entry level positions, while incorporating extensive skill development and promotion opportunities.

One of Curt's sales managers, Craig, describes a conversation he had with his son. "Dad isn't it interesting how passionate you get about work." As he reflected on this he realized, "It used to be that work was just a job for me. Now, am I passionate? You bet, and I feel it acutely. Each day I try to see my customers get reliable, accurate equipment that will give many years of quality service, and maximize the money they spend. Should our meters fail, the chemical spills into the environment, or worse, causes injury to someone's father or mother, someone's friend. I don't just build and sell products, I am taking care of my neighbors and friends."

> **Connecting our work to ways it contributes to making life right for others deepens our passion and joy about what we do.**

OVERCOMING FALSEHOOD, NOURISHING TRUTH

The economic and material ways in which businesses can do justice are obvious and life-critical. Businesses can also address equally important, but less visible contributions to people flourishing. One is by working to overcome some of the falsehoods that defile human life and economic relationships. Four lies distort the lives of rich and poor alike. Business is a holy calling when it contributes to replacing these lies with truth. These lies suggest to those who are poor that they are worthless, helpless, and hopeless. They seduce those who are financially better off into believing that their assets shape their worth and future.

Economic Lies		Business Truths
The lie of ownership: "It's mine"	**Replaced by**	We are stewards of the products and services that contribute to well-being.
The lie of net worth: "I'm nothing" or "I'm important"	**Replaced by**	We work to affirm the worth of all creation, and provide products and services worthy of our life in God's image
The lie of hopelessness: "I'm trapped," "The future is bleak," "The powerful elite will always win"	**Replaced by**	We nourish hope by ensuring everyone has access to the resources and relationships needed to flourish
The lie of mere benevolence: "Giving is an optional act of kindness from excess"	**Replaced by**	We give to others as an act of grace in action, and to be reminded that God owns all things

For Reflection and Discussion

What's your reaction to the assertion that business has a role in overcoming "economic" lies?

How does this contribute to the implementation the perspectives in the previous chapters that business must be done with the regard to being surrounded on all sides by the sacred?

1. Overcoming False Ideas of Ownership

Both those who are comparatively rich and those who are relatively poor can be deceived into believing they have the right to totally control "our possessions." All of us have an urgent need to give a portion of our possessions away in order to avoid being possessed by them. Unless we live in the freedom of knowing that God owns our resources, "our" things will own us. All people—even those in poverty— need to give in order to be freed from idolatry. God's strongest judgments against Israel focused on condemnation of their failure to give to the poor and oppressed. It is right, good, and essential to work to earn an income. However, we also need to work to deliver one another from trusting our money and possessions as our sources of security. Think of how many advertising campaigns provoke greed, envy, and insecurity.

A sober illustration of the price of false notions of ownership is woven into the history of Haiti. In the decade prior to its 12-year long war for independence that ended in 1804, Haiti was listed as the world's richest colony. In the over two centuries since its independence, Haiti has ranked near the bottom of the world's poorest nations. What went wrong? The answer isn't found if we only look at education, health, or culture. We need to look at business—and more specifically, to the lie of ownership.

As a price for victory in their revolt as slaves, and the price they had to pay to France to recognize their independence, Haitians were forced to pay millions of dollars for France's loss of "property"— including slaves. It took 122 years, until 1947, often amounting to 80% of the government's revenue, to pay this ransom and its accrued interest. No wonder roads, schools, hospitals and other vital infrastructure have been so poorly developed. The misuse of power and the corruption Haitians experienced as slaves built a culture of corruption within the country.

In order to discourage other slaves from staging a similar revolt, the US and many European countries imposed total trade embargos. This further deepened Haiti's economic catastrophe. The US didn't recognize Haiti as a nation for 60 years, partially out of concern that American slaves might be inspired by the Haitian revolution and start their own "insurrection" (fight for freedom). These embargos and several US military occupations have been reinstated throughout Haiti's history in response to dictators and coups.

When there were no embargoes, Haiti was self-sufficient, and actually a net exporter of rice and sugar. In 1994, through the IMF and World Bank, the US led an effort to renegotiate Haiti's international debt. But this came at a high price. The cost was Haiti accepting free trade for products from the US. As a result, millions of tons of US subsidized sugar and rice were exported into Haiti, undercutting farmers and making Haiti the US's third largest market for rice. Now the primary export crop for Haiti is mangos, which aren't exactly a high volume, high profit crop.

In response, development organizations, and some businesses recognize that economic investment by governments, NGOs, and businesses is an act of justice, or reparations. Creating meaningful work that contributes to people flourishing in Haiti is an act of making life right. [76] Private/public business partnerships are emerging that are intentionally focused on providing the economic opportunities for Haitians to secure well-being.[77]

We are born into situations with unfairly balanced, even unjust, scales. Businesses unavoidably create and shift resources along that scale. God's will is done when this occurs in ways that ensure the balances become fairer and people's lives flourish. In other words, the result is movement towards equity—justice. Business is a holy calling when it works to ensure that the balances in the marketplace

---

[76]For an economic history of Haiti see Paul Farmer and Noam Chomsky, *The Uses of Haiti* (Courage Press, 2005) Randall Robinson, *An Unbroken Agony: Haiti, from Revolution to the Kidnapping of a President* (Basic Civitas Books, 2008); and in fiction, Isabelle Allende, *Island Beneath the Sea* (Harper Collins, 2010 reprint).

[77] See for example the work of Technoserve: Business Solutions to poverty. www.technoserve.org. See also Michael Fairbanks, "A business solution to poverty in Haiti," *Christian Science Monitor*, July 12, 2010.

are fair, the wages and payments are just, and the integrity and honesty of the transactions are secure. God is especially concerned with how those who are vulnerable to others' exploitation are protected and safeguarded in our business activities.

For Reflection and Discussion
What's your response to this portrayal of an aspect of Haiti's economic history? What do you see to be the role of business in helping create "fair balances?"

Possible Implications for Business: *Working to promote trade regulations, labor practices, working conditions, and access to economic opportunity isn't secondary to business. Even when these dynamics make doing business more complicated, and maybe more costly, we can pursue this with confidence, knowing that the adoration we give God in Sunday's worship services, is matched by the business services we provide the rest of the week.*

2. Overcoming False Ideas of Worth
Another sinister lie to which business can directly speak is the false notion that bank balances measure a person's net worth. I cringe when I hear people refer to someone who is wealthy as a "high net worth individual." Our things aren't the source of our worth, identity, or power. People without financial resources aren't "nothing," with low net worth. People with large balances aren't of greater worth than others. Yet, for example, families of victims from the Malaysian Airlines Flight 370 crash are being compensated in drastically different amounts, depending on nationality. Malaysian relatives are likely to receive around $5,000 each, Chinese as much as $1 million, and American relatives between $8 to 10 million.[78]

Overcoming the lie of disparate human worth is rarely quick or simple. Think of how long it may take in our own life to believe that

---

[78] "MH370 families face huge compensation disparity," *CNBC Business News* (March 25, 2014).

our worth isn't defined by our performance, accomplishments, acquisitions, and others' affirmation. How hard it is for us to believe, really believe, that we are unconditionally loved by God?[79]
Since our heart is found wherever our treasure is located (Matt. 6:21), our heart is chronically at risk if our treasure is money, material goods, or our own abilities. If business encourages trust in a product, experience, or service as the key to happiness it risks promoting heart disease. If I allow my engagement in business to fuel my greed, my pride, my ambitions, or finding my net worth in financial statements, I am at risk of heart disease. God knows our need for security—that is why God calls us to place our trust in God and not things. God knows our need for a sense of worth— that is why God invites us to discover our identity as beloved sons and daughters.

Pope Francis proclaimed, "When power, luxury and money become idols, they take priority over the need for a fair distribution of wealth. Our consciences thus need to be converted to justice, equality, simplicity and sharing."[80]

In one of the saddest statements a person can utter, one man quietly said to my wife and me during a meeting with landless farmers in Nicaragua: "We are nothing. A farmer without land is nothing. When we're hired we work hard on other people's land. They gain all the profit. We barely earn enough for today, but have no chance of getting ahead or helping our children have a better future. We are trapped. We're willing to work hard, but unless we gain access to land of our own to farm, we will remain nothing." We were visiting on behalf of the land reform NGO, Agros International that has been working in Central America for several decades, providing

---

[79] For further reflections on this, see Tim Dearborn, *Beyond Duty: A Passion for Christ, a Heart for Mission,* (Dynamis Resources, 2013). For an analysis of the implications of grace for economics, see Kathryn Tanner, *Economy of Grace,* (Fortress: 2005).
[80] Pope Francis, *Message of Lent* (2014).

loans to farmers to buy land in cooperative villages. [81] There is a degree of sociological truth in the landless farmer's words. To be poor isn't simply to lack the resources required for life. True poverty is to lack *access* to those resources; it's to be without the relationships or opportunities to gain what is needed for well-being. Agros, like many other NGOs and businesses, works to make the balances more fair.

Christians in business work to both affirm the intrinsic worth of all people, and to enable them to gain access to the goods and services that will contribute to their flourishing. All people are

Affluence can seduce us into linking our worth to our wealth. Business as a holy calling works to free us from false identities.

creatures of unimaginable worth, unique, unrepeatable miracles of God's creative goodness.

Possible Implications for Business: *Poverty and under-employment can make one feel like nothing and feel trapped, with no way forward. Business exists to create access to livelihood, including new and restored relationships and opportunities. Without this, poverty drains all possibilities from people's lives.*

For Reflection and Discussion
Most of us don't feel very rich—for we can always compare ourselves upward to those who are better off financially than we are. Check out and discuss your response to this ranking of where you are on the global income scale: www.globalrichlist.com. What's your reaction to where you are on the global income scale?

3. Overcoming Hopelessness
Both those with wealth and those in poverty are tempted to succumb under the weight of despair, fear, or isolation. Cynicism and skepticism press down hard; leading people to conclude that there is no way out, no hope, and no options. Corruption,

---

[81] See www.agros.org

incompetence, trade barriers, the magnitude of need, environmental problems, systemic conflict, and others' greed are ugly facts that lead to the conviction that there is nothing we can do.

People in poverty are sometimes driven to fear and desperation. People may be tempted to believe that the only reason they are poor is because others are rich. Substance abuse taunts people as an escape. For some, violence and migration seem the only way out of their prison to secure a future for their children. Impoverished people are willing to go thousands of dollars into debt to those who might smuggle them into Europe or North America, leaving their children behind as collateral on the loan. Parents are willing to sell a child into prostitution. Acts of sheer desperation!

The drive to migrate for a better life won't be stopped by higher walls.

It will diminish as: businesses establish economic opportunity,

the natural environment is restored,

trust and the rule of law return to public squares,

decades of economic injustice are rectified, and

people see hope blossoming at home.

Higher barriers, tougher laws, or militarized borders won't resolve the migration of desperate people seeking sanctuary and livelihood in a foreign country. Walls and deportation won't stop the flow of refugees and economic migrants. This depends on establishing safe communities and sustainable livelihoods in the countries people are fleeing.

People in affluence are sometimes driven to fear and isolation. It's obvious—but nonetheless surprising. Greater affluence doesn't necessarily produce greater contentment. In fact, some of the loneliness, most anxious, and most fearful people in the world rank high on the "Global Rich List." Even someone at the Federal poverty level in the U.S. ranks among the top 2% of the world's wealthiest people. It is ironic that America, the land of the free and home of the brave, and one of the most affluent nations in the world's history, would have its public political debates filled with language of fear, defensiveness, and anger.

Walls, security systems, higher barriers, and stronger defenses seem the only way to stem threats to their affluence and secure the future for their children. For the affluent also, substance abuse and other addictions offer destructive escapes from feeling isolated.

God's purpose for business speaks directly to this. "The main purpose of individual businesses and commercial systems is…addressing genuine human needs through the creation, development and production of goods and services; organizing good and productive work; using resources to create and share wealth and prosperity in sustainable ways."[82] Business is consistent with God's will and ways when it seeks to treat all life in ways that honors its "sacredness." This implies very specific, very concrete action. It's not a vague ideal. The theologian Elizabeth Johnson comments, "The fundamental sin is exploitation, whether it be expressed in the domination of male over female, white over black, rich over poor, strong over weak, armed military over unarmed civilians, human beings over nature."

Equal employment opportunity, equal wages for equal work, commitment to care for those on the margins, and protection of the environment, are all ways business serves its purpose of guarding the sacredness of life. To do this requires an economic structure in which those who possess economic (and military/political) power don't, as Johnson asserts, insist on their superiority and assume they have the right to exercise dominative power over all others for their own benefit.[83]

---

[82] *Vocation of the Business Leader,* 13.
[83] Elizabeth Johnson, *She Who Is* (Crossroad Publishing, 2002), 27-28.

Possible implications for business: *Business includes among its purposes providing people with solid reasons for hope through access to the goods, services, and to the meaningful opportunities to earn a living that they need to further their well-being.*

4. Contributing to a Fair Balance

There is a common lie that if I give some of "my" money away I can do with the rest whatever I want. This stems from the lie of ownership. Biblically, as has been explored in this study, we own nothing. God owns it all. Therefore, we give away just as we spend, as conscious acts of obedience and stewardship.

God's example and God's word declare that sharing our resources is

> We give, not only to care for others, but to remind ourselves that we love God and we love others, trust God and care for others, more than we love and trust "our" financial resources.

a mandatory act of obedience and a worshipful act of love. As Paul says in 2 Corinthians 9:7: *"Each of you must give"*—not just those with wealth, but everyone. And each gives *"not reluctantly or under compulsion,"* but *"because of the surpassing grace of God that has been given to you"* (v. 14). Our faith is tested by whether or not we are generous. God is glorified by our giving (2 Cor. 9:13). Both those with abundant resources and those without enough have a need to give and to receive—not just for the sake of the poor, but also for the sake of our own souls. And we give in *"that there might be a fair balance"* (2 Cor 8:13-14).

The Latin root of the word *charity* literally means "grace-in-action" and *philanthropy* literally means "love for humankind," Grace-in-action, active love for others! When we give to help others gain access to the resources they need to flourish, we are mobilizing grace and love. We are not simply mobilizing financial resources.

Those with resources have as much a need to give, as those who are desperately poor need to receive. Similarly, those without financial resources have rich gifts to give—that they need to be given the opportunity to share. Since we exist in the image of the God who gives, giving is woven into our humanity.

It's easy to be tempted to believe that giving is an optional addition to our lives. Charity often occurs as an exceptional, superabundant, voluntary act of benevolence, given from excess or abundance.[84] However, we know that deep damage can be done to the character of both donor and recipient when some are reduced to beggars seeking spare coins, and others are reduced to mere benefactors bestowing those coins.[85]

There is a life and death urgency in the world for business to contribute to making life right. Therefore, churches have an urgent, life-critical need to help Christians in business understand and work in ways that are consistent with God's will. Skills, wisdom, resources, and energy can be applied through business to address some of the complex issues that contribute to poverty and injustice: global business practices, access to life-giving innovative technology, basic services, educational and health innovations, and even our own vocation, personal consumption and lifestyle.

All people need to give in order to experience the joy of being fully human.

---

[84] There is an inverse correlation between giving and income in the US. Those earning under $50,000 per year give on average 4% of their income to charity. Those earning between $200,000 and $250,000 give 2.4%. http://nccs.urban.org/nccs/statistics/Charitable-Giving-in-America-Some-Facts-and-Figures.cfm, and *The Chronicle of Philanthropy,* October 2014. In terms of the % of the population that regularly gives to charity, Americans rank 13th in the world. 62% for the US, with Myanmar the highest at 85% and the UK 2nd at 76%. https://philanthropy.com/article/Americans-Rank-13th-in/153965.

[85] See Steve Corbett and Brian Fikkert, *When Helping Hurts: How to Alleviate Poverty without Hurting the Poor…and Yourself* (Moody, 2014).

Possible implications for business: *Giving can be an act of justice, making life right, leveling the playing field (a form of Jubilee), creating access to resources and providing restitution for past wrongs. Thus businesses have a vital role in this through courageous ventures that may not produce as high a profit margin but contribute to life being made right.*

For Reflection and Discussion

How do you respond to objection that an emphasis on justice pushes the role of business too far? How would a conversation go with a colleague about the assertion that your business could contribute to a fair balance, stop "destructive exports," and guard people's hearts?"

Personal Strategies for Catalyzing Change. What do I believe God is calling me to do within my sphere of responsibilities to contribute to justice: life being made right for others?

	Strategies for catalyzing change
Interests: What interests me about how work can contribute to justice—making life right?	
Sphere of responsibility: How can my role contribute to this?	
Ways to model the change I value: What can I do immediately?	
Concerns outside my responsibility: What issues and opportunities are outside my role?	
Key people: How can I build key relationships to encourage and support others in their spheres of responsibility (in areas about which I'm concerned)?	
Prayer: For what can I pray?	

If you want to evaluate this and strategize your response further, see *Evaluating How My Business and Work Participate in God's Purposes*

6. Integrity: Ensuring Trustworthiness in the Vulnerable Places of Society

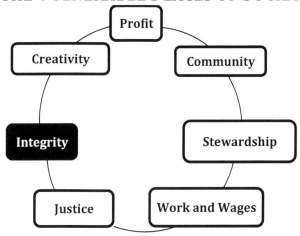

This section examines the qualities God nourishes in people in order to shape businesses that help weave trustworthiness into the fabric of society.

By the end, participants will be able to summarize the implications for management, marketing, and competition when integrity is pursued as one of the purposes of business.

CENTRAL QUESTION: How does the notion that one of God's purposes for business is to build integrity into society enhance your appreciation for and evaluation of what you do at work?

Todd and Scott are brothers who believed that their business had a purpose beyond making paper products for a profit. They wanted their employees to flourish and their customers to receive a helpful, quality product at a fair price. They believed business should honor the individual regardless of his or her role, provide an opportunity to grow within the organization, hold fair dealing as the norm, celebrate frequently, and share the fruit of people's labors with the entire staff. They also were committed to hiring physically and mentally challenged employees whenever the nature of the work permitted it. Through the years they found that employees felt like partners because they were treated like partners.

As a result, employees worked like partners who understood that, in business, profits are not guaranteed but must be "built." Each team member played a role in that process and by working diligently, cooperatively, and creatively the financial bottom line would thus be healthier. This would mean that there would be more to share.

The culture was one of respect and grace. The company understanding was, "The cost of a mistake is the tuition we pay in the school of hard knocks. Let's learn from mistakes and move on." The upside was that employees were then free to take educated risks without fear. The brothers shared the profits with the entire staff. They also were committed to sharing a portion of the profits philanthropically, to care for others in contexts of poverty. This further motivated everyone. Employees had a say in corporate philanthropy and were proud to see that their work was benefitting others both by the work they produced, and by the profits they could give away.

Of course, this culture of sharing increased operating costs. Competing with offshore manufacturers whose wages, benefits, environmental care, and operating costs were less placed them at a competitive disadvantage. Domestic manufacturing of paper products was a comparatively high cost enterprise. One option was to send their manufacturing off-shore, but that would require laying off domestic team members who helped build the company. This was not an acceptable choice. Todd and Scott committed themselves to protecting the jobs. The team members appreciated that deeply, this enhanced morale, and caused everyone to pitch in to seek greater efficiency and productivity. Todd praises God for the ways God honored their approach to business. Their company survived the 2008 economic downturn and continues to flourish.[86]

Nourishing Trust and Honor

As we've asserted, business has access to people's lives at very vulnerable points, often in places that Christian ministries can't reach. People's needs, desires, and fears surround most business transactions. How these are addressed leaves an impact on the well-being and character of individuals, as well as the well-being and character of society as a whole. One of the purposes of business is to nourish trust, honor, and dignity, and to deepen integrity in the fabric of society. Integrity isn't simply an issue of business ethics. It's an essential dimension of business purposes.

Integrity Defined: Integrity means soundness, wholeness, and completeness. To have integrity is to be without hidden deceptions.

One purpose of business is to build integrity into the fabric of society.

Integrity creates a safe, reliable place where people can put their weight down. That's why when God calls people through the Old Testament prophets to live faithfully; some of the first signs of integrity and even faithfulness to God are trustworthy scales, honest contracts, and fair prices, payments, and wages. (See for example, Leviticus 19:36; Proverbs 20:10, 23; Micah 6:11; Isaiah 3:14-15; 5:7-9; 58:3.)

This study has proposed that these aren't merely expressions of HOW business works (ethics), but of WHY it exists (purpose). A society in which people's word can't be trusted, people's contracts aren't binding, and people's portrayal of their product and services

---

[86] www.riteintherain.com.

are phony is unstable. If a business relies on corruption, greed, and graft to succeed, then society, and especially people without power, languish. Isaiah proclaims that the Lord is *"appalled"* when *"truth stumbles in the public square"* (Isa 58:14-16).

E-commerce flourished in its first decades because people assumed transactions could be trusted. Products were accurately represented, goods would actually be shipped, and credit card information wouldn't be scammed. Every time we use a credit card we are at risk of fraud and identity theft. Without integrity, non-face-to-face business transactions are especially precarious.

I find the tagline of Old Dominion Freight Line fascinating: "Helping the World Keep Promises." Their CEO, David Congdon, writes, "A lot of people think OD is in the business of shipping freight...What we're really in the business of doing is keeping promises." They don't view their cargo as "just a bunch of cardboard boxes" for "each one contains promises," and "we believe the world runs on promises." What a great description of a business linking its work to a grand purpose of integrity—helping the world keep promises.[87]

Questions of integrity surround every transaction:
- Will the product or service be reliable?
- Will it provide what the customer needs?
- Has the product been truthfully represented?
- Will the transaction be trustworthy?

---

[87] www.odfl.com

For Reflection and Discussion

What do you think about these questions of integrity?

1. Are the desires that the product or service claims to satisfy worth fulfilling?

2. Does the product or service have a good impact on the customer's life, as well as on creation itself both now and for coming generations?

3. Will the desires our product or service fulfills nourish the customer's character, dignity, and relationships with others; or are they demeaning and unworthy of people's lives in God's image?

Integrity is deepened when the product does what we claim it will do, and lasts as long as we promise. When it doesn't, we do what is necessary to set things right. The transformation in customer service, and "no questions asked" return policies among retailers in the past decades demonstrates this good (though costly) commitment to integrity.

This is also dependent on integrity in the customer. Recreational Equipment, Inc. had to make their return policy more specific, limiting returns to one year after purchase. Customers had been returning hiking boots after four years of use, complaining that they were wearing out. Up until this policy change, REI refunded money for any purchase, any time, for any reason.

To explore how business contributes to infusing society in its vulnerable places with integrity, we will examine three of, what for many, are the most awkward aspects of business for Christians: integrity and management, integrity and performance reviews, and integrity and marketing and competition.

Managing with Integrity

We are called to be servants in Christ (1 Cor 4.1; Phil 1.1, etc.). The first are last, the least are greatest (Matt 19.30). We are all brothers and sisters without barrier or hierarchy. How, therefore, do we manage (and be managed) by others, in ways that honor our dignity as equals, meet organizational objectives, and fulfill God's purposes?

When I taught at the University of Aberdeen, in Scotland, one of my students experienced the painful reality of what it means to be treated as a servant, and the dis-integration of life that can cause. He took a summer job as a servant in a Highland castle. He spent his day making sure the lords' and ladies' boots had the mud scraped off when they came back from hunting and fishing. He promptly took their coats and gave them tea (or whiskey) when they came in the door. He addressed them all by title, responded to their every need, and had continuous, face-to-face contact with them every day. Sunday was a shock when he sat next to them in church, now equals before the Lord, and none of them recognized him. Granted, few of us may be, or have servants. But I wonder if there are people that I treat as objects or mere providers of services, rather than as persons?

People aren't merely units of production, overhead costs, or sources of services, or of income. Managing staff isn't simply about maximizing productivity. Management with integrity is about stewarding people, time, talents, and resources. Management is integral to business as a holy calling, for managers are directly engaged in that which is sacred.

1. Management with Integrity Begins with Vision

How we manage is determined by how we view our team, the purposes of our work, and ourselves. In other words, our vision shapes our approach to management. If I see people, time, talents, and resources merely as means to other ends—productivity, attaining targets, maximizing profit, and getting the job done—then both people and integrity are likely to be put at risk. If I see the importance of what we do, as well as how and why we do it, then I will be on the road to managing with integrity.

Management with integrity isn't about techniques; it's about seeing a clear and compelling purpose for what we do. Max De Pree comments, "One examines leadership beginning not with techniques but rather with premises, not with tools but with beliefs, and not with systems but with understandings."[88] When we manage with a clear vision for how our business participates in God's purposes, then we are more likely to lead with confidence and grace.

"People with a vision inject ambiguity and risk and uncertainty into our lives. They embark on voyages to new worlds."[89] Risk can be scary for some managers and employees, since by definition it is out of control. Old school patriarchal management focuses on implementing hierarchical systems of control based on authority, supervision, rewards, accountability, and duty.

When a manager's vision includes confidence in God's interest in their work, they then can lead knowing that their lives are indeed "out of their own control." When they believe that God is also concerned about their business and the people they serve, then they can be more comfortable with ambiguity, confusion, and change.

2. Management with Integrity Depends on Character

The effectiveness of our management depends on the quality of our relationships, and our relationships flow from the quality of our character. If there isn't soundness, wholeness—in other words, integrity—in our inner being, it is unlikely there will be integrity in our outer actions. Our character both shapes, and is shaped by our behavior. Effective managers embody the values and commitments

---

[88]Max De Pree, *Leadership Jazz* (Doubleday, 1992), 7.
[89]De Pree, 40.

they advocate for their staff. Peter Block documents in *The Empowered Manager* that, "If top management wants to create a vision or set of values for the organization, let them create it and live it out for themselves first for two years or more. Then let them worry about how to engage others in the vision. Stop enrolling, start embodying."[90]

A former President of Alaska Airlines would occasionally show up in overalls, unannounced and without any introduction, as a new member of the plane cleaning crew. His goal was simply to understand what the job was like and to find ways to enhance employee job satisfaction and performance.[91] He also wanted to model the corporation's value of "building a diverse and inclusive company where everyone feels valued, committed, and connected."

> **Hypocrisy: when perceived behavior doesn't coincide with professed values.**
>
> **Integrity: when actual behavior coincides with professed values.**

I invited students in an MBA course I was teaching to conduct an audit of their organization's integrity as it relates to its official vision and values statements. Are these simply archaic management exercises that don't shape corporate behavior, or do they really matter? Each student interviewed people who were managers, non-management staff, customers, and suppliers, showing each the corporate vision and values. They asked each person to describe areas of alignment, and also ways the organization could become more consistent. As is to be expected, the results were very diverse, but the exercise provoked fruitful conversations.

---

[90]Peter Block, *The Empowered Manager* (Jossey-Bass, 1987), xv.

[91] This kind of engagement has now been popularized in the Emmy Award winning reality TV show "Undercover Boss" that is in its 6th season.

For Reflection and Discussion
Examine the vision and core values statements of your organization.

Discuss the degree of consistency between your organization's actions and these official affirmations.

What helps and hinders you to embody these commitments in your work?

3. Management with Integrity Requires Integrating Care for People and Concern for Productivity

Management is concerned with both persons and productivity. Much management literature such as by Covey and Block is based on the assumption of the inherent goodness of people.[92]

This is true, but the biblical faith adds more. We believe people are good for we are in the image of God, but also prone to selfishness and deceit. How do we encourage the best in people, help people surmount potential selfishness and deception, and not become skeptical, critical, control, and restraint-oriented in our approach to management?

For nearly a decade I managed a highly motivated, very diverse team of 16 people from 12 nationalities living in 12 different countries. We all had leadership roles in an organization with 45,000 staff who worked in 95 different countries. Our team only met together as a group for a few days each year. The rest of my "management" of them was done remotely. Each person brought immense competence, differing convictions and perspectives, and strong passions to our team. Integrating strong, talented, and gifted

---

[92] Stephen Covey, *The 7 Habits of Highly Effective People* (Simon and Shuster, 2013). In addition to *The Empowered Manager*, see by Peter Block, *Community: The Structure of Belonging* (Berrett-Koehler, 2009), *The Answer to How is Yes* (Berrett-Koehler, 2003), and *Stewardship: Choosing Service Over Self-Interest* (Berrett-Koehler, 2013).

persons around common goals to maximize both community and productivity required constant effort. I learned wonderful insights from this team. Working with them was also an opportunity to learn about management in complex workplaces and organizations. Some things I learned about management include:

Agree upon and stay focused on clear goals and objectives. It is demoralizing and divisive to be unsure where you're going or to be pulling in different directions. Your objectives can be time-specific and re-evaluated at an agreed upon date. But to continually change direction is disempowering for a team. Your job as a manager is to keep people focused. They all "work for you" in regard to your teamwork toward common objectives.

Agree on team "norms." Build an agreement about how you will work together, disagree, and communicate. Your job as a manager is to help maintain this.

Be honest about your own limitations. Affirm that others may know more about particular areas than you do. In their areas of specific responsibility, you "work for them" to help them succeed.

In conflict, stay focused on building understanding. The initial goal isn't resolving the conflict, reaching agreement, or someone winning. The initial goal is to make sure everyone feels heard and understood by the group, and that you've benefited from diverse and conflicting insights.

- Help everyone understand why people have the convictions they hold.
- Create an environment in which differences aren't threats or criticisms.
- Keep the group focused on the group's goals and agreed norms.
- Guard against suppressing conflict, or forcing your view. It's not about an individual winning, but about the group succeeding.

Agree on time-bound plans. In light of your agreed goals, and the insights that have been shared by the group, adopt a time-bound plan for how to move forward in next steps toward your goals. Agree on a date when you will re-evaluate. Between then and now, stay focused on your agreed next steps.

Tolerate and learn from failure. If you want a team that is open, collaborative, and creative, then you must be willing to allow mistakes and failure. Determine what are reparable and what are irreparable failures. In all situations, help people to admit their mistakes, discern the causes, address the consequences (to the extent possible), and determine what can be done in the future that will lead toward a better outcome.

A new employee at a large company made a massive mistake in his first month, costing his company over $1 million. He was called into his boss' office, sure that he was going to be fired. His boss asked a series of questions about what had happened, why it happened, what he learned from this, and what could be done differently in the future. After this, his boss abruptly said, "You can go now." Sure that his boss meant, "You can leave, you're fired," he thanked his boss for the month they'd been together and expressed regret that he hadn't worked out and needed to leave. His boss replied, "Leave? We can't afford to fire you. You're our most valuable employee. We've just invested $1 million in your training."

> Experience always teaches. But it's not true to say it is necessarily a "good" teacher.
>
> Properly reflected upon experience that leads to changed understanding, attitudes, values, and behavior is a "great" teacher.

4. Management with Integrity Involves Leading as a Follower and Following as a Leader

Change often begins (and usually gets lived out) at the bottom of an organization. Therefore, effective managers find ways to lead from below. This includes allowing those whom they lead to have a say in the direction of the organization. However, that invitation also requires those "being led" to share responsibility for the consequences of decisions and actions.

Peter Block comments that, "The power of position is overrated. We frequently find people near or at the top feeling as powerless as people in the middle or at the bottom."[93] It's not always true that "the direction and culture of an organization are created by the people at the top."[94] As we've asserted throughout this study, people at all levels in an organization can contribute to shaping the culture of the company and enhances the organization's work. This correlates with Jesus' assertions that *"the first shall be last," "the greatest shall be the least," "don't seek a position of honor,"* etc.

To manage well, ask the questions followers ask. Similarly, followers are wise to ask the questions leaders ask:
- What may I expect from you as the leader—and from you as a staff member?
- Can I achieve my goals by following, and working with you?
- Will I reach my potential by working with you?
- Can I entrust my future to you?
- Are you prepared to lead—and to follow?
- Are you trustworthy?

People are motivated by the affirmation. Simple acts of appreciation can be nourishing. Regardless of our position in an organization, whether a manager or not, all people can lead through honest and sincere affirmation of co-workers. This is explored thoroughly by Gary Chapman and Paul White who have developed a training and

---

[93]Block, 63.
[94]Block, xviii.

organizational assessment program for "Motivating by Affirmation."[95]

This can also be implemented through basic actions such as:

- Write a personal note of appreciation to a staff member or co-worker every week.
- Regularly affirm good performance.
- Help others around me achieve their goals.
- Encourage staff training and development opportunities.
- Learn from my own mistakes and encourage others to learn from their own.[96]

Regardless of our position in an organization, we can practice the transformational advice given by the Apostle Paul, *"Whatever is true, whatever is honorable, whatever is just, whatever is pure, whatever is pleasing, whatever is commendable, if there is any excellence and if there is anything worthy of praise, fix your mind on these things"* (Phil. 4.8).

Management with integrity nourishes a sense of individual responsibility and even authority. Followers want to have their lives and input count, but that means sharing responsibility for the consequences. "The payoff for dependency is that if we act on someone else's choice and if it does not work out well, it is not our fault. Dependency is the wish not to be responsible and held accountable for our actions or our direction."[97]

Of course it's vulnerable to trust others, especially when we are held accountable for the outcomes of others' actions. As De Pree says, "Delegation requires a form of dying, a separation of issue from

---

[95] Gary Chapman and Paul White, *The Five Languages of Appreciation in the Workplace* (Northfield, 2012).

[96] For more see Ted Engstrom, *The Art of Management for Christian Leaders* (Zondervan, 1989), 164.

[97] Block, 107.

self. We must surrender or abandon ourselves to the gifts that others bring."[98] Delegation is the prerequisite for both a work style that is life giving, and a work environment that nourishes creativity.

For Reflection and Discussion
How do you evaluate yourself, your own manager, and your team in light of the qualities discussed in this section?

Who is someone you respect or admire who could guide you into greater fruitfulness as a manager (and follower)?

What steps would you like to take?

CONDUCTING PERFORMANCE REVIEWS WITH INTEGRITY
How does integrity get expressed in an employee performance review? I once was visiting an office in Asia and the air was palpably filled with awkward tension. I asked the Human Resources manager what was going on and she indicated it was performance review week—and everyone hated it. Managers as well as their staff felt awkward dealing directly with reviewing individuals' work and contribution.

Done from the perspective of business as a holy calling, employee performance reviews can be a vital opportunity to participate in God's purposes (and the specific purposes of the organization) in people's lives. Rather than being merely an act of judgment or accountability, performance reviews can be an opportunity to reflect and learn through experience—and discern how and if this particular position is appropriate for the individual and team.

Rather than being a tension producing, awkward time that strains relationships, encourages competitive rivalry among co-workers, and

---

[98]De Pree, 157.

123

deepens anxiety—"performance review season" can be a time of growth, encouragement, and team building.

Questions for staff performance reviews
To do this, it helps to approach performance reviews with some of the same questions and attitudes that we bring to interviews when we are first considering hiring someone. Who would not want to be asked the following questions, and how could they do anything other than contribute to someone's growth:

1. What have been your goals/objectives? To what extent have you met them? What's helped, hindered? What would you do differently?
2. How have you grown professionally? What next steps of growth would you like to take? What further training and experience would be most helpful?
3. What do you need from me as supervisor to maximize your work?
4. What are the greatest strengths you bring to your work?
5. What challenges are you currently facing that would be helpful for me to know about?
6. How do you evaluate the quality of your relationships with colleagues?
7. What do you think those who work with you would say about your contribution?
8. What are the dominant emotions you feel about work? What would you hope to be feeling about work 6 months from now? What can we do to move toward that?
9. What's the greatest contribution you think you could make to the organization over the next year? What's necessary to free you to do that?
10. If you could change/delete/add anything to your job description, what would you want to change? What impact would that have on your team, on the organization?

For Reflection and Discussion

Have you ever had a manager who demonstrates these kinds of qualities? What was particularly impactful on you?

Whether or not you are in a position as a manager and team-leader, "the inmates run the prison." Everyone has a role in shaping the work environment. What ideas do you have for how you can work differently to create a grace-shaped community?

MARKETING AND COMPETING WITH INTEGRITY

1.   Turn the Other Cheek and Beat Out Competitors?

How do we turn the other cheek, go the extra mile, give to the one who asks from us, and live knowing that the last will be first and the first last—while at the same time succeeding in a highly competitive marketplace? Does following Jesus' sayings about "*loving our enemy*," and "*doing to others what we'd want them to do to us*" involve sharing our trade secrets, letting others secure deals ahead of us, or telling customers the weaknesses of our products and services?

It's no wonder we've often gained the impression that competition is unspiritual and that marketing is manipulative. Yet competition is intrinsic to most cultures—if not as individuals, at least as families and groups. Competition is overtly or subtly a driving force in many organizations. Even churches aren't exempt from competing with one another for members and influence (all done in the "name" of serving God of course).

If competition is basic to many dimensions of life, might we benefit from more sermons outlining a theology of competition? The tension (and guilt) generated by serving and struggling in competitive workplaces is a consuming reality that leaves some businesspersons feeling unclean and not knowing how to wear their business clothes and their faith at the same time. For what should they pray? "Lord, help me to beat out my competitors?" "God, may I succeed at closing this deal before another company gets it?"

"Father, whatever it takes, help me to grow this business and to advance in my career." These prayers don't sound like they align very easily with the gospel.

We are surrounded at work by systems of rewards and punishments. The criteria are usually fairly clear. Some companies even grade their employees on a bell-curve. For everyone on a team who gets a 5, someone must be ranked at the bottom, receiving a 1. Promotions, raises and continued employment depend on this. Some companies lay off the bottom performing 10% of their work force every year—seeking to fuel internal competitiveness and drive for excellence.

For Reflection and Discussion
How would you rewrite the prayers for success in business that are mentioned above in ways that might more fully reflect God's purposes for business?

What are the positive values in competition? When is competition "bad" and "unchristian?"

What would it look like to honor and "love" "competitors?"

What would happen if you wrote notes of encouragement to other staff, or even other "competitors" when they did well, affirming them for their success, their sales, or the contracts they've been awarded?

2. Compete for Good Reasons
Why are we in business? Whom are we serving? In what do we trust? Do we trust our own efforts as if everything depends on us? Or, do we trust the faithfulness of God? Are we competing against other people? Or, are we competing against ourselves—always seeking to be the best we can be to the glory of God? In other words, are there insights from Jesus that would enhance our effectiveness as competitors in the workplace—or would his ideas bring disaster? What insights does the Gospel provide for how to approach business competition?

126

Track coaches admonish their athletes not to look around to see where they stand in relation to other runners. Rather, they need to stay focused on their own running and on the finish line. To turn and look will slow you down and likely bring disaster.

Similarly, some of the best golfers comment that they stay focused on the course, not on their standing against other players. They see themselves primarily as competing against themselves, trying to improve their own skill and performance. Rowers have a special advantage in racing shells. They are facing backwards in the shell and can't even see the goal. Their concentration is primarily on their own effort and on staying harmonized with their rowing mates.

Recently, my wife and I were cycling with two of our grandchildren, ages 2 and 4. My wife started out first with the two year old on her bike. I got going with our four-year old grandson. Looking ahead, he saw that my wife and his sister were ahead of us. "We better go fast Papa so that we can catch up," he said. And his reason wasn't because, "we want to be first." Rather, his statement stunned me. "We don't want them to be up there all alone."

You might be thinking that this sounds fine for recreation and grand-parenting, but not amidst the hard, competitive demands of business. If I don't get there before my competitors, I lose. If I'm not available 24/7 to service the needs of customers and clients, they'll go elsewhere. However, when we compete for good reasons, we can also compete with confidence and courage.

3. Compete with Confidence and Respect

We begin once again with the recognition that we are not dealing only with finite resources. Our purpose is not merely to serve our employer, our customers, or our own financial needs. We serve the trustworthy God whose concern for our own and others' flourishing far surpasses anything we can imagine.

Jesus reminds us in Matthew 6:33 not to worry about what we'll eat, wear or possess. God is faithful. Rather, we seek first God's kingdom. So we return to the insight that we're surrounded by the sacred—people, time, and material things—all belong to God and stem from God's hand.

Criteria for respecting our competitors. There are some clear implications for competition and marketing:

- We do not try to prove the value of our product or service by putting down our competitors.
- We do not say anything negative about them, or their product.
- We do not misrepresent our own or others' products or services to give the impression that what we have to offer is better than they are.
- Our goal is to connect people with goods and services that will satisfy their needs at a cost they can afford and will provide for our business. It might be best at times to direct potential customers elsewhere in order to find what they need. This could contribute to deepening people's appreciation for our business and nurturing long-term customer loyalty.

4. Compete with Contentment and Dignity

As we've said, business creates a great opportunity *not* to define our worth by achieved targets and goals. Our worth is defined by God's love. It's easy to slip into only seeing our own failures and inadequacies; attentive to the ways we've messed up. It's no wonder that "fear, loneliness, and envy" dominate so many people's emotional lives. Imagine the impact of God producing the fruit of the Spirit in our competitive, comparison-oriented, self-judging and self-justifying souls?[99] No wonder, after listing the fruit of the Spirit,

---

[99] For a fascinating study of the relationship of the fruit of the Spirit to professional performance reviews see, Al Erisman and Denise Daniels, "*The Fruit of the Spirit: Application to Performance Reviews,*" Christian Business Review (August 2013), 27-34.

Paul goes on to admonish us not to *"compete against, or envy one another"* (Galatians 5:22, 26).

My wife was meeting with a group of female leaders in Korea. When they discussed promotion and people being selected for senior leadership positions, one made a striking comment. "But if I was promoted I'd leave other women behind and violate our support of one another as a group." That's not a concern voiced very often by Western, dominant culture males. I know, at least, that I'd never even thought it. This led to a fascinating conversation about using increased power and influence to benefit others, rather than simply for one's personal gain.

In order to safeguard our approach to competition, some of the key biblical perspectives we've explored provide parameters to erect around our behavior:

- Are we stewarding the sacredness of all we touch: people, time, money, resources, the name and glory of God?
- Are we providing the best product or services possible at the best price possible to satisfy real needs in our customers and our business?
- Are we contributing to life being made right for others?
- Are we becoming the best people we can possibly be through this work?

Consider the implications of this for advertising. What is our impact on potential customers when we use discontent or provoke the desire for things people didn't know they needed as marketing tools? My wife and I were visiting an Arctic village in Alaska the week the first television arrived in the village. Most of the village clustered in the one house with a TV. The ads were as impactful as the show. After watching the dismay of a homeowner when his dog strayed across spotless tile floors with muddy paws, for the first time, the Eskimos' plywood floors seemed less satisfactory. We are straying away from guarding the "sacredness" of people when we market our products or compete with others in ways that undermine their sense of worth.

Criteria for evaluating products and services. The following criteria are proposed as consistent with the biblical faith to use in evaluating products and services:

- Does this product do something positive to enhance people's physical, relational, or emotional life?
- Does this product use resources efficiently? Does its disposal create significant issues?
- Does this product create new problems?
- Does our way of marketing this product have a virtuous impact on the life of potential consumers (provoke positive, life-giving desires, attitudes, and behaviors)?

For Reflection and Discussion

How relevant are these criteria for marketing and competition in your own situation? What's your response to the following: *"Advertising...promotes dissatisfaction with the status quo in an endeavor to get you to purchase a particular product. Is stimulating discontent with the status quo...compatible with biblical principles? [Our] economy thrives on change and new products...Getting people to switch products because of some dissatisfaction with their old one is a legitimate function of advertising. When such changes enhance people's well-being, I believe it is appropriate to promote dissatisfaction with the status quo, and I can see nothing wrong with this from a biblical perspective."*[100]

---

[100] Thomas Dunkerton, "Biblical Principles Applied to Advertising" in *Biblical Principles and Business: The Practice,* Richard Chewing, editor (NavPress, 1990), 96-7.

Personal Strategies for Catalyzing Change. What do I believe God is calling me to do within my sphere of responsibilities to personally work with greater integrity and to nourish integrity within our business?

	Strategies for catalyzing change
Interests: Which aspects of integrity as a purpose of business interest me the most?	
Sphere of responsibility: How can my role contribute to nourishing integrity?	
Ways to model the change I value: What can I do immediately?	
Concerns outside my responsibility: What issues and opportunities are outside my role?	
Key people: How can I build key relationships to encourage and support others in their spheres of responsibility (in areas about which I'm concerned)?	
Prayer: For what can I pray?	

If you want to evaluate this and strategize your response further, see *Evaluating How My Business and Work Participate in God's Purposes*

7. Creativity: Nurturing Organizations with Creative Vision

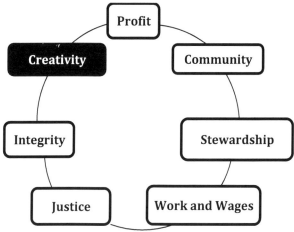

This section examines ways to unlock innovation and creativity in business, in order to contribute to people and all of creation flourishing.

By the end, participants will be able to identify ways to receive more fully from God gifts that will enhance their own creativity, and will encourage it in their business and church.

CENTRAL QUESTION: How does the idea that God is interested in inspiring creativity in your work impact your perspective? Are there ways you've seen God do this?

Don wanted to enhance both the morale of his automobile business's mechanics and the quality of their customer service. Often customers complained of feeling somewhat mystified by what had been invisibly done to repair their car, and by the incomprehensibly large bill they received. Mechanics felt like extensions of socket wrenches, pushed to improve efficiency. Rather than convening a management meeting to figure out from the top how to solve this problem, Don hosted a lunch for all the mechanics. When he asked for their ideas to improve their customer relations, a flood of ideas poured out.

Within a week, the garage and their customer satisfaction were transformed. Rather than the service manager explaining to customers what had been done to their car, the mechanics themselves walked their customers through what they'd done. Rather than the sales department calling the customer the next week to make sure everything had gone well, the mechanics were paid as part of their job to call the people on whose cars they had worked. Mechanics' pride and dignity, and sense of responsibility and authority soared. Customer satisfaction and loyalty became solid.[101]

RESTORING CREATIVE VISION

1. A Mark of the Spirit

Peter's sermon to the crowds in Acts 2 at Pentecost describes the power of vision in God's purposes. He quotes from the Prophet Joel, who proclaims Israel's messianic hope about the Spirit inspiring dreams and visions among all people—regardless of age, gender or social class. God pours out the Spirit on people, not merely for gratifying spiritual experiences, not merely for tongues of fire, not merely for miracles—but for creativity and vision.

---

[101] For more on this see Don Flow, "How do you live faithfully?" *Faith and Leadership,* Duke University (Feb. 15, 2010). www.faithandleadership.com/qa/don-flow-how-do-you-live-faithfully.

One mark of the presence of the Spirit of God on the people of God is the capacity to dream dreams, to see visions, and to live with creativity. The same Creator Spirit by whom all of life was called into existence is now at work within God's people—manifesting the same extravagant creativity as in the beginning.

The world needs bold people freed by God's radical love and empowered by the creativity of God's Spirit to dream dreams and see visions. We need well-equipped men and women who are flooded with confidence in the loving sovereignty of God. Mako Fujimura suggests that one of the first questions that should be asked whenever we enter church is "How does God want to create something good and beautiful through you?"[102]

We need to nourish a vision for our business and organizations (even our church congregation), by asking: "How can we participate in some small way in signs of heaven coming to earth now, here, in this place, through us?" All creativity depends on vision. What we see depends on where we look. Ignatius of Loyola said, "Strive to keep before your eyes your one and only goal, that is the greater service and glory of God."[103]

2. The World is Desperate for Dreamers

Dreamers have always led the world. Throughout history two forces have driven "radicals": dismay with the present and a vision of a better future. They have abandoned the values of their era's *status quo* because of a passionate belief that life could be better. The 'possible' appeared to them as such an improvement over the 'actual' that no amount of sacrifice, suffering or insecurity was too high a price to pay in its pursuit. Driven by a dream, people have been willing to topple governments, overthrow corrupt religious

---

[102] For his reflections on creativity see Makoto Fujimura, *Culture Care*, (Fujimura Institute, 2015).

[103] Ignatius, *Monumenta Ignatiana: Epistolae et Instructiones*, (Madrid, 1903-1911), 1:720.

establishments, launch new businesses, reform social institutions, explore new realms of science, journey to unknown lands, and pursue life-transforming technological innovations. The world will never be the same because of these dedicated dreamers.

If we look only at the world, we will be overwhelmed by its needs and our inadequacies. The Old Testament theologian Walter Brueggemann says, "The dominant values of our culture, as they are embodied in economics [and] military policy...are values of hopelessness."[104] In contrast to this—we have the capacity of the Spirit to provoke creativity—and inspire solid reasons for solid hope. Creativity can be celebrated, regardless of the creator. It's obviously not a quality confined to Christians.

Business thrives on creativity, and creativity thrives on dreamers who can envision something new, and are curious about how things can be done differently.[105] Our world is shaped by creative innovations that envision new and better ways to respond to deep needs. We've explored the dramatic impacts of cell phones. Imagine a world without internet or electricity. Someday life without genetic therapy for cancer and other illnesses will be unimaginable. Life still dependent on fossil fuels for power will seem archaic.

Most people live from the present toward an uncertain future. Creative people bring the future into the present.

---

[104] Walter Brueggemann, *Hope within History* (John Knox, 1987), 7.

[105] For brief reflections on this, see, Colin Baird, "Why You Should Always Nurture Curiosity," *CEO.com* (July 11, 2014), www.ceo.com/entrepreneurial_ceo/why-you-should-always-nurture-curiosity/. For longer studies on creativity in business see, Michael Michalko, *Cracking Creativity* (Ten Speed Press, 1998); Mihaly Csikszentmihalyi, *Creativity: Flow and the Psychology of Discovery and Invention* (HarperCollins, 1996); Gareth Morgan, *Imaginization: The Art of Creative Management* (Sage Publications, 1993); and Evertt Rogers, *Diffusion of Innovations* (Free Press, 1983).

We are more likely to see life as God sees it, when we allow the Spirit to shape our imaginations and draw us into the life of Christ. God's vision propels us into the world with the twin prayers of *solidarity* with God's broken heart ("Let my heart be broken with the things that break the heart of God,"[106]) and *anticipation* of God's coming kingdom. *"Thy kingdom come and thy will be done on earth as it is in heaven"* (Matt 6:10). We live in the

The Spirit empowers us to give tangible evidence of the reality of hope and expose the lies of despair.

certain confidence that all authority in heaven and earth has been given to Jesus (Matt 28:18)—that includes authority over science and commerce, technology and financial systems. Nothing is excluded. And one day, all suffering and sorrow will cease and all life will be united in God's great love. So we live in courageous revolt against all that is contrary to God's will and ways, and are empowered by the Spirit to demonstrate tangible signs of that coming day.

Our vision is for God's kingdom to fill the earth, and for our lives and our world to be transformed by God's sovereign love and clothed with God's gracious goodness. This relates to our physical, material, economic life—just as much as it does to our spirituality.

3. The Future Has Invaded the Present

The capacity of Christians to live with joyous hope while being fully engaged in the harsh realities of our world—even the, at times harsh, competitive and complex realities of business—is one of the most compelling signs of God's kingdom.

I believe that the people of God are entrusted with all the resources needed for the world to flourish. Everything. All the finances. All The vision. All the creativity. All the capacity. Name a need that thwarts flourishing—poverty, waste disposal, corruption,

---

[106] Written by Bob Pierce, the founder of World Vision, on the flyleaf of his Bible in 1950 upon viewing the devastation of the Korean War.

unemployment, trade barriers, inadequate education, water shortages, environmental degradation, incurable diseases and intractable conflicts—and I believe that God has entrusted to the global Christian community everything we need to resolve it. Into our societies and business that often feel trapped by insufficiency, God sends his people, filled with the same Spirit that made the world in the first place. *"I will send the Spirit who will lead you into all truth, and through whom you will do even greater works than I have done"* (John 14:12; 16:13). Greater works than the Creator! It sounds almost blasphemous—yet such is the promise of the One in, through and for whom all things are created.

For Reflection and Discussion

What's your reaction to this?

How do you see its relevance for your life at work, and particularly for business?

This is not something we do strenuously or on our own. Rather, we have the joy and gift of simply being the unique person we were created to be and walking in the good works that God has prepared for us. *"For we are God's workmanship, created in Christ for good works, which God prepared before hand to be our way of life"* (Eph. 2.10). There is nothing that restricts these good works to church-related activity. God wants heaven to invade every aspect of earth.

> Our work in the world isn't simply to make a living, turn a profit, and do a little good. It is to participate in the Spirit of God clothing the whole world in the goodness of God's love.

When we look at the world with God's eyes of grace, we recognize that God's purpose is not simply to make our sin-stained lives more manageable, but to make us completely better—the end result of the process we usually refer to as "transformation". Julian of Norwich, the 14th century English anchorite, was shown that the gift of grace is to discover that we are enclosed in the goodness of God.[107]

4. Learn to Listen to the Right Voice

I have learned through years of sleepwalking to recognize the gentle voice of my wife over the noise of my dreams. Spiritually, I am learning this through years of listening each morning for God's voice through scripture. Recognizing the right voice comes through familiarity, through daily practice. But knowing who is speaking is only part of the journey. Trusting what is said comes next, and then obeying. Learning to trust that the voice we hear is good and that we will receive the strength to obey is the journey of grace.

Unlike the assertion that work is about violence to the body and spirit, work can actually be fun. A sense of playfulness can permeate even otherwise mundane jobs.

When our work is done according to God's will and ways, it may actually feel like play.

Christmas shoppers in 2014 at an Edeka store in Germany were startled into joy when the checkout counter workers broke into a synchronized rendition of "Jingle Bells" using the tones on their electronic scanners.[108] Besides the original customers, within a week over 4 million people had watched the video on-line.

Rather than our about work being clouded by fear, loneliness, and envy—creativity, joy, contentment, and even fun—can permeate work. [109] Increasingly, employers are recognizing that staff are motivated by far more than money. A sense of purpose, the

---

[107] See for example, Julian of Norwich, *Revelations of Divine Love*, in *The Complete Julian of Norwich* (Brewster, MA: Paraclete Press, 2009), 83.

[108] See http://www.flixxy.com/jingle-bells-on-grocery-checkout-scanners.htm

[109] Dennis Bakke develops this from his own experience of success and failure in business in *Joy at Work: A Revolutionary Approach to Fun on the Job* (PVG, 2005).

opportunity to grow, the capacity to contribute, and enabling others' lives to be better motivate most people—because we are created in the image of the God. One participant in a *Business as a Holy Calling?* group commented recently that even if he wasn't paid to do his work and didn't need to earn an income, he'd still do it.

At an international symposium of psychologists on creativity and its cultivation, Carl Rogers, the renowned psychologist, proclaimed that one of the most desperate needs in society…is "for the creative behavior of creative individuals…The great shadow which hangs over us all necessitates creative responses."[110]

5. Creativity Isn't Determined by Our Abilities and Resources
Our creative capacity does not flow from our areas of evident strength and giftedness but from the life of Christ in us. The Creator of all life, who made everything out of nothing is not handicapped by our weaknesses and difficulties.

God's Spirit works mightily within us to release and express the life-giving, creative presence of God in the midst of our fallen world. Theologian and musician Jeremy Begbie describes this by saying that the "Spirit enables and propels the dynamic process of creativity in humankind. The act of creating something, the cultural act, can

> "The hope of faith must become a source of creative and inventive imagination in the service of love." Jürgen Moltmann

therefore be spoken of as a 'spiritual act'."[111] This is not merely about renewing the original creation but about the birth of God's

---

[110]Carl Rogers, "Toward a Theory of Creativity," in *Creativity and Its Cultivation,* ed. Harold Anderson (New York: Harper and Row, 1959), 69-70.

[111]Jeremy Begbie, *Voicing Creation's Praise* (Edinburgh: T. & T. Clark, 1991), 5, 179.

new creation.[112] It is the foretaste of a future that will bring forth more than was possible in the old creation.

Typically we associate creativity with art, and more specifically, with what we do outside of work (our hobbies, gardening, recreation, etc.) Yet creativity is integral to all aspects of life, and especially business. Think of the impact of the simple invention of Post-it Notes, or the more complex development of waste digesters to generate fuel and fertilizer. These began with curiosity and vision. Or, moving from physical products, think of the impact of creative forms of communication. Facebook has grown in its first ten years from a college dorm room to nearly 1.4 billion monthly users (almost 20% of the world's population in 2015). Or, think of Google, that also was born in a college dorm room, launched in 1997 in a garage, and in 2015 has almost 1.2 billion users. Or think of a company that doesn't produce many products of its own. It vision is to make other companies products more accessible. In its first 20 years (to 2015), Amazon has grown from a Seattle garage to global distribution sites that "carry" 200 million products, has over 240 million regular customers, and a quarter of a million employees.

For Reflection and Discussion

What are other examples from your own experience of ways innovation in business express creativity?

Seattle Pacific University conducts an annual social venture competition among its undergraduate students. The winners receive grants to implement their business ideas. The creative business responses to pressing social needs that these students have developed are remarkable. In recent years these include a business to develop a portable refrigeration unit for vaccine storage in rural

---

[112] See Kerry Dearborn, *Drinking from the Wells of New Creation* (Cascade Books, 2014). See also, Jurgen Moltmann, *Religion, Revolution and the Future,* 112.

contexts, a home-based sewing business for immigrant women to create high end garments for major retail stores, a bakery employing people who are homeless to get them off the streets at night and to help them learn job skills, a business creating high quality prosthetic feet from used tires for amputees in developing countries, and a kinetic powered light and water purification system.[113]

For Reflection and Discussion

How does this assertion relate to the ways you actively rely on God's engagement in your business and work?

What possibilities does this open up for how you approach challenges at work?

God the Creator, through the vision-inspiring Spirit can flood our imaginations with new insights into what is possible. Our acts of creativity are participating in God's great creation and new creation. The presence of Christ with us through the Creator Spirit frees us to be the center of creativity for the world. Rather than being a stronghold of commitment to security and the *status quo*, the people of God are creatively enabling positive change.

BUILDING COMMUNITIES OF CREATIVITY

The international symposium of psychologists on creativity that was mentioned earlier identified several prerequisites for creativity that have always been affirmed in the gospel and that are still urgently needed today.

1. Sense of Personal Worth

Confidence in our unconditional acceptance by God can encourage creative engagement with the painful realities of the present. Carl Rogers found that recognizing that one's worth is not controlled by

---

[113] For more on this see www.spu.edu/acad/school-of-business-and-economics/SVPC.html.

the evaluations of others, or even by one's performance, is an indispensable prerequisite for creativity. He refers to this as the condition of "psychological safety," acceptance of an individual as a person of unconditional worth. [114] As Christians, our lives are marked by the "safety" of God's grace, knowing that we are accepted and of worth because of God's life on our behalf in Jesus Christ.

For Reflection and Discussion
What would a sense of acceptance and worth look like in our businesses?

2. Integrated Character
This is the result of what psychologist Abraham Maslow describes as the end of the "inner war within each person. To the extent that creativeness is constructive, synthesizing, unifying, and integrative, to that extent does it depend in part on the inner integration of the person."[115] He stresses that all discussion of creativity must begin with the personality of the creative person rather than with the person's achievements. He refers to essential "characterological qualities" of creative people – such as boldness, courage, freedom, spontaneity, integration and self-acceptance. [116] As Christians, we recognize these qualities as the work of the Spirit in our lives.

For Reflection and Discussion
What could our business activity do to nourish these character qualities in both employees and customers?

---

[114] Rogers, "Toward a Theory of Creativity,"76–78.
[115] Abraham Maslow, "Creativity in Self-Actualizing People," in Anderson, *Creativity and Its Cultivation*, 88.
[116] Maslow, 93.

3. Curiosity

Creativity depends on curiosity and the ability to enter into life with all its complexity. One must hunger and thirst to know more. The philosopher and psychologist Erich Fromm wrote, "The capacity to be puzzled is indeed the premise of all creation."[117] Think of the number of times you've felt puzzled at work, not knowing what to do or how to resolve a situation. That's actually a good gift, an essential prerequisite for creativity.

A lack of openness to the future and to change – in other words, a lack of faith and hope—may nurture desperation but does not feed creativity. Fromm asserts that creativity requires "willingness to be born every day...to be creative means to consider the whole process of life as a process of birth, and not to take any stage of life as a final stage. Most people die before they are fully born. Creativeness means to be born before one dies."[118]

For Reflection and Discussion

How can we encourage curiosity, honor good questions, and affirm the desire to explore new ways of working in our business?

4. Freedom to Fail

Creativity depends on being willing to go where others do not go, to be regarded as foolish if need be, and even to make mistakes.[119] When we live from one center, Jesus Christ, before only one audience, God the Father, and know that God is for us, delighting in us, then we are on the road to greater freedom from our fear of failure.

The grace of God empowers us to face life boldly, diminishing the control exercised by the threat of loss. In Christ we have already

---

[117]Erich Fromm, "The Creative Attitude," in Anderson, *Creativity*, 48.
[118]Fromm, 53.
[119]Rogers, "Toward a Theory of Creativity," 77–79.

both lost and gained everything. *"I have been crucified with Christ; and it is no longer I who live, but it is Christ who lives in me"* (Gal. 2:19-20). *"I regard everything as loss because of the surpassing value of knowing Christ"* (Phil. 3:8). Yet, *"All things are yours, whether...the world or life or death or the present or the future—all belong to you, and you belong to Christ"* (1 Cor. 3:21-23).

Living this isn't easy. I recently spoke with friend who is a partner in an investment management company. With the consent of his clients, he invested 5% of their portfolio in high risk ventures. He was reasonably confident this would produce great results. Instead, it was disastrous. He was overwhelmed with shame, failure, and the loss of few clients.

This has provoked great pain, lots of reflection, and deep growth. Rather than paralyzing him in caution, and crippling him with shame and guilt, this has drawn him closer to an identity in God's unconditional love, given him new insights into investments, and deepened his courage. Risk, loss, and change need not terrify or control us. Fromm believes the life of creativity requires courage and faith. "Without courage and faith, creativity is impossible, and hence the understanding and cultivation of courage and faith are indispensable conditions for the development of the creative attitude."[120]

For Reflection and Discussion

In what ways do we make it safe for people to fail, and even reward good—but unsuccessful—efforts?

What is your work situation like in terms of building these qualities required for creativity?

---

[120] Fromm, "The Creative Attitude," 54.

These four qualities create a powerful bridge between Christians and all people, regardless of their religious convictions:

- *sense of worth,*
- *inner peace and integrity,*
- *curiosity, and*
- *freedom to fail*

Possessing these qualities doesn't depend on faith. They are expressions of how God created all people to live. Therefore, we can affirm and praise these qualities in all people in which they are found. They are the result of life in God's image. However, the gospel undergirds and deepens our confident ability to live with this kind of visionary, bold, creativity.

PROVIDING THE WORLD WITH SOLUTIONS

A sense of worth, character integrity, curiosity, and the freedom to fail are integral to life in Christ. These qualities deepen in us as the Spirit forms and recreates us more and more fully into the image of Christ. As a result, we are called and empowered to live this way in all our interactions in the world. When others are searching for a solution to a complex political, social, economic or medical problem, the people of God should be first in line to offer hope and potential solutions. People of God provide "a creative contradiction to this dying world";[121] living in joyous rebellion against all that keeps us from becoming what God intends us to be.

Businesses have the opportunity to demonstrate by the quality of our community what is right and life giving and healing. To people who perceive themselves to be trapped by their own or others' actions, by lack of access to essential resources, or by being cut out of the market for economic livelihood, business is set into action. We have the privilege of exercising every means God gives to set

---

[121]Moltmann, *Religion, Revolution and the Future,* 119.

people free from all that dehumanizes, defiles, or threatens to destroy their humanity.

This is the kind of compelling vision for business that will enable employees to look forward to going to work in the morning. This is the kind of work that will enable us all to come home in the evening satisfied and content. In some small way, in our corner of the world, we enabled something good to come into people's lives and into the rest of creation.

This is business as a holy calling. Businesses are positioned as some of the prime organizations to connect people with life-giving, life-sustaining resources. God's Spirit gives us vision, courage. and creativity to help connect people with the resources of God to help them and all of creation to flourish.

For Reflection and Discussion
What's a dream or vision I have for what more God could enable me/us to be and do in business (or the support of people in business)?

Personal Strategies for Catalyzing Change. What do I believe God is calling me to do within my sphere of responsibilities to be more creative, encourage creativity in our business, and encourage creativity in our society?

	Strategies for catalyzing change
Interests: What intrigues me in the assertion that a purpose of business is to nourish creativity among workers, customers, suppliers, and society?	
Sphere of responsibility: How can my role encourage creativity?	
Ways to model the change I value: What can I do immediately?	
Concerns outside my responsibility: What issues and opportunities are outside my role?	
Key people: How can I build key relationships to encourage and support others in their spheres of responsibility (in areas about which I'm concerned)?	
Prayer: For what can I pray?	

If you want to evaluate this and strategize your response further, see *Evaluating How My Business and Work Participate in God's Purposes*

Conclusion: Business as Radical Discipleship

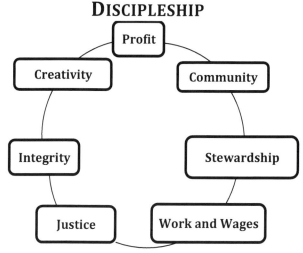

> **This section** integrates everything explored in this study and offers some exercises for businesspersons and pastors to discern the next steps they'd like to take.
>
> **By the end,** participants will be encouraged to evaluate both their own engagement in business, and their own work life to see how it can be improved to participate more fully in God's will and ways.

"When we cry, 'Abba! Father!' it is that very Spirit bearing witness with our spirit that we are children of God, and if children, then heirs, heirs of God and joint heirs with Christ." Romans 8:16–17

Of course business is measured by income generation, return on investment, and profitability. Profit is essential for businesses, perhaps even more so for small businesses with less access to capitalization in the event of a down cycle. But profit only is a means, and only one indicator of how we are contributing to the flourishing of people and all creation.

Both profit and not-for-profit organizations exist to serve communities' and people's needs. Financial profit, like charitable contributions are essential means to other ends—but very insufficient ends in and of themselves. As has been asserted throughout these reflections, income growth is too small a target, too inadequate a scorecard for Christian businesspersons.

Business is far more significant in God's purposes than warrants reducing the measures of fruitfulness to profit and sales. Our scorecard must be bigger than profit margins and sales targets.

Many businesses are now pursuing "triple bottom line" audits—auditing not only their financial accountability, but also their accountability with stakeholder communities and care for the environment. This is a great improvement over doing business with only profit as our purpose. In this study we've explored not just 1 or 3 bottom lines, but seven purposes that God would nourish in a business if it's to be fulfilled as a "holy" calling. Even if we're not in a position to influence the overall purposes of our business, we can allow the Spirit to shape the purposes of our own work life and engagement in business.

To support and equip Christians in business to work faithfully toward these "bottom lines" requires intentional and even radical discipleship. The challenges are great. The answers aren't easy. Jesus' command in Matthew 28 declares that God calls us to participate in Christ's transformation of everything!

"And Jesus came and said to them, 'All authority in heaven and on earth has been given to me. Go therefore and make disciples of all nations, baptizing them in the name of the Father and of the Son and of the Holy Spirit, and teaching

them to obey everything that I have commanded you. And remember, I am with you always, to the end of the age.'" Matthew 28:18–20

If we seek "to obey everything that Jesus commanded," then we need also to pay attention to all that he said regarding money, competition, how we treat our enemies, ambition, and caring for those who are poor. Nothing escapes the domain of his authority. This does not simply pertain to our personal and spiritual life, but to our public, business and even political engagement as well. Are we building community, deepening dignity and honoring people in our approach to business? Are we helping people to receive an identity that is defined by affluence and possessions, or by their inherent worth and identity as children of God?

God intends to bring every dimension of life under the gracious authority of Christ—and that includes business.

As we pray, *"Our Father, thy kingdom come and thy will be done on earth as it is in heaven,"* we are not simply praying for the salvation of our souls, but for the transformation of our societies.

Businesses have a remarkable capacity to participate in the coming of the God's kingdom and to contribute to the transformation of society—but it won't happen accidentally or automatically. It requires intentional strategies and radical discipleship. Pope John Paul II stated that the purpose of business "is not simply to make a profit, but is to be found in its very existence as a community of persons who in various ways are endeavoring to satisfy their basic needs, and who form a particular group at the service of the whole of society." An inherent characteristic of work is that "it first and foremost unites people. Therein lies its social power to build community."[122]

If Christians in business are going to contribute to this, their churches need to be dedicated to equipping and supporting them. For business to be a holy calling, it needs to be done as a form of sacred stewardship, for as we've seen, we are surrounded by the sacred. The commands of God run against the current of many common practices and require courage, creativity, and a supportive community. The costs of not doing this are grave and the rewards for faithfulness are great. Christians in business have the need and opportunity to gather together in communities of radical discipleship. Churches have a vital role in helping form such groups for their members who are engaged in business.

If I misuse the resources entrusted to me, I am squandering someone else's inheritance.

If I mistreat the people around me, I am harming someone in God's image.

If I encourage people to place confidence in possessions, I am promoting idolatry.

It is so easy to become focused on the mechanics of producing, marketing, buying and selling that we miss the bigger and deeper bottom-lines and benchmarks of success and impact.

The ultimate measure of the ministry of business is deep change in our lives—suppliers, customers and staff alike. These relationships create a quality of community that transcends culture and context. When these relationships include our guardianship of creation— then even the trees of the field will "break forth into shouts of joy" at our coming (Isaiah 55:12). We have the privilege of being used by

---

122 John Paul II, Encyclical Letter *Centesimus Annus*, 35; and *Laborem Exercens*, 20; cited in *Vocation of the Business Leader*, 18.

God to provide the world today with clear evidence of the coming kingdom of God.

"For surely I know the plans I have for you, says the Lord, plans for your welfare and not for harm, to give you a future with hope." Jeremiah 29:11

Concluding Reflections for Businesspersons

1. What insights from this study have you found particularly helpful? (You might want to review anything you wrote as "Personal Strategies for Catalyzing Organizational Change" at the conclusion of each chapter).

2. What questions still remain?

3. What specific steps do you think God is guiding you to make in order to bring your own work-life into closer expression of God's will and ways?

4. How can we support one another more fully as we seek to live out business as full-time ministry, and what can we do as a church to assist in this?

5. For what would you like prayer?

Concluding Reflections for Church Leaders

As you reflect back on this study, are there any changes you feel called to make in regard to:

1. Your vision for your church's ministry?

2. How you engage with the occupational and business lives of your members?

3. The next steps you would you like to take to continue to engage with businesspersons to pursue business as a holy calling?

Concluding Evaluation of Expectations

Review the summary you wrote of your initial expectations when you started this process (page 37).

To what extent have your expectations been met?

What next steps do you want to take?

COMMISSIONING AND PRAYER

This can be used at the conclusion of your group to pray for one another. It also could be incorporated into a retreat, fellowship group or church worship service.

Leader (Pastor or Facilitator):
In Jesus Christ, we are all called into full-time Christian ministry, and given gifts for a variety of service for the common good. In the ministry of your daily life and work, will you seek to do all to the glory of God, and participate in God's will and ways being done on earth, as in heaven?

I will.

In your daily occupation, will you seek and pray to steward all you encounter as sacred, for the people, time, and resources you serve and use belong to God?

I will.

In the vocation to which God has called you, will you pray for wisdom, courage, and power to do work for justice, integrity, and creativity to be nourished in society?

I will.

Let us name before God all the occupations we represent, as expressions of our ministry in God's kingdom:
Each person names his or her occupation(s).

Let us pray. (Prayer can be said in unison, by the leader, or by participants taking turns praying).

Father, be present with us where we work. Deliver us from idolizing our own effort, and being driven by fear and envy. Empower us to be faithful stewards of your good gifts.

Holy Spirit, guide and strengthen us to to carry on our work in ways that contribute to all people and all of creation flourishing.

We give you thanks for all forms of service:
for those who farm and provide the food we eat,
for those who guard and nurture creation,
for those who labor in factories, mines, mills, and stores,
for those who care for the sick and research new cures,
for those who invent and explore, compose and create,
for those who manage finances and records,
for those who provide leadership and governance,
for those who market products and for those who transport them,
for those who teach, nurture, and inspire,
for those who clean and maintain, and who protect and defend,

Just as your creation is abundant, so you have given us abundant ways to serve you as fruitful stewards.

Guard the dignity and well-being of those who are unemployed, retired, or disabled. Strengthen and guide them in your ways of service. For those who need caregivers, provide people who care with competence and kindness.

Creator God, you are the source of our life and labor. May you be honored and glorified in all we do.

Give all people access to the resources they need to enhance dignity, community, and flourishing.

We ask this trusting in your unfailing love, and your presence with us in the power of the Spirit through Jesus Christ our Lord, Amen.

EVALUATING HOW BUSINESS PARTICIPATES IN GOD'S PURPOSES

Part 1 Community

Reflect on your particular business and your role within it. To what extent are you participating in this particular aspect of God's purposes? Though each person's role in shaping the overall purpose and culture of a business is limited, everyone, regardless of their position, has some influence. See the section, *"Catalyzing Organizational Change."* NOTE: It is assumed that you will not discuss specifics of your business in your business integration group. It might be helpful for you to seek the personal counsel of your pastor.

How does my business, work, (or for pastors—church) contribute to community?	Reason for evaluation
Community Are positive, caring human relationships developed in ways that bridge differences between people?	
1. How do I/we evaluate my/our relationships with co-workers? *Strained Difficult Good Very Good* 1 2 3 4	
2. How do customers describe the quality of the interaction they have with me/us? *Abrupt Cautious Competent Trustworthy* 1 2 3 4	
3. How do vendors/suppliers and competitors evaluate interaction with us? *Strained Difficult Good Very Good* 1 2 3 4	
4. How do investors and funders evaluate the transparency, and responsiveness of my/our engagement with them? *Weak Some Acceptable Excellent* 1 2 3 4	

Part 2 Stewardship of Time and Money

Does my business (and do I) steward resources well?	Reasons for evaluation
Stewardship Does our business (and my own lifestyle) steward people, capital, natural resources, and the environment in ways that honor God's will?	
1. Do I/we exercise wise use of financial capital? *Poor Industry Standard Good Excellent* *1 2 3 4*	
2. Do I/we engage in sustainable use of natural resources and mitigate our impact on the physical environment? *Poor Industry Standard Good Excellent* *1 2 3 4*	
3. Do I/we encourage (and demand) a day off each week, and appropriate vacation and leave? *Poor Industry Standard Good Excellent* *1 2 3 4*	

Part 3 Stewardship of Work and Wages

Does my business provide meaningful work and fare wages?	Reasons for evaluation
Work and Wages Does our business treat and pay employees fairly, providing meaningful work that contributes to the provision of legitimate human needs?	
1. Am I/are we treated and paid fairly? *No Industry standard Above Avg Excellent* *1 2 3 4*	
2. Have I/we provided meaningful work that provides for legitimate human needs? *Tedious/Worthless Ok Interesting Satisfying* *1 2 3 4*	
3. Do I/we produce high quality, efficiently provided goods and services? Quality: *Poor Industry Standard Good Excellent* *1 2 3 4*	

4. Efficiency: *Poor Industry Standard Good Excellent* 1 2 3 4	

Part 4 Justice

Does my business (and do I) contribute to justice?	Reasons for evaluation
Justice Are people—employees, customers and competitors—treated with dignity in ways that contribute to life being made right?	
1. Do I/we treat all people affected by our work fairly? *Rarely Sometimes Usually Nearly Always* 1 2 3 4	
2. Do I/we contribute to the generation and distribution of honorably earned income? *Not sure Industry Standard Usually Yes* 1 2 3 4	
3. Do I/we provide opportunities or even charitable giving that provides for those who can't compete or attain a sustainable livelihood? *Not sure Industry Standard Some Regularly* 1 2 3 4	
4. Do we have a system in place to monitor and report incidents and grievances that violate our values or treat people unfairly? Do I feel comfortable using it? *No Yes but barriers Yes but stigma Safe and Trusted* 1 2 3 4	
5. How often do I/we evaluate our supply chain and the treatment of workers/the environment involved in the provision of the goods/services we use? *Never Rarely Occasionally Frequently* 1 2 3 4	

Part 5 Integrity

Does my business (and do I) deepen integrity in every interaction and thus in society?	Reasons for evaluation

Integrity Are qualities of honesty, kindness, and trustworthiness nurtured in the characters and interactions of all who are affected by this business?

1. Employees? *Rarely Sometimes Usually Nearly Always* 1 2 3 4	
2. Customers? *Rarely Sometimes Usually Nearly Always* 1 2 3 4	
3. Suppliers? *Rarely Sometimes Usually Nearly Always* 1 2 3 4	
4. Funders? *Rarely Sometimes Usually Nearly Always* 1 2 3 4	
5. Competitors? *Rarely Sometimes Usually Nearly Always* 1 2 3 4	

Part 6 Creativity

Does my business encourage creativity among our employees and in society?	Reasons for evaluation
Creativity Is "creation guarded, ordered and rendered more fruitful," innovation encouraged, and creative responses developed to create products, services, and a better work environment that satisfy legitimate human needs and contribute to people and nature flourishing?	
1. Do I/we feel like my/our creativity and insights are honored and expressed? *Rarely Sometimes Usually Nearly Always* 1 2 3 4	
2. Does our organizational culture encourage and reward innovation, while ensuring an appropriate degree of the freedom to fail? *Rarely Sometimes Usually Nearly Always* 1 2 3 4	
3. Can I/we see ways in which we contribute to people and creation flourishing? *Rarely Sometimes Usually Nearly Always* 1 2 3 4	

For Reflection and Discussion

Review your responses to the evaluation of how your business and work participate in God's purposes that you've completed at the end of each section. There is a copy of the entire evaluation in the Resource section.

1. In which areas do you give your business (and work) the highest rating? What can you do to celebrate with others the areas in which you are strong?

2. Which areas did you rate below a "3"?

3. Why did you make this evaluation?

4. What do you learn from this?

5. Based on this assessment, are there any things you would like to do to align your work more fully with God's purposes?

6. What immediate steps do you think you could take?

7. How would you like others to pray for you in this?

RECOMMENDED RESOURCES

Jeff Van Duzer, *Why Business Matters to God and What Still Needs to Be Done to Fix It* (Intervarsity Press, 2010)

Kenman Wong and Scott Rae, *Business for the Common Good: A Christian Vision for the Marketplace* (InterVarsity Press, 2011).

Also:

Robert Banks, *Faith Goes to Work: Reflections on the Marketplace* (The Alban Institute, 1993).

David Bapstone, *Saving the Corporate Soul.* (San Francisco, Jossey Bass, 2003).

Richard Chewing, John Eby and Shirley Roels, *Business Through the Eyes of Faith* (Harper San Francisco, 1990).

Drew Cleveland and Greg Forster, *The Pastor's Guide to Fruitful Work and Economic Wisdom* (Made to Flourish, 2014).

Stephen Graves and Thomas Addington, *The Fourth Frontier: Exploring the New World of Work.* (Nashville, Word Books, 2000).

Timothy Keller, *Every Good Endeavor: Connecting Your Work to God's Work.* (Riverhead Books, 2014).

Ched Myers, *The Biblical Vision of Sabbath Economics* (2001).

Michael Novak, *Business as a Calling* (Free Press, 1996)

Laura Nash, *Believers in Business* (Nelson, 1994)

Laura Nash and Scotty McLennan, *Church on Sunday, Work on Monday* (Jossey-Bass, 2001).

Tom Nelson, *Work Matters: Connecting Sunday Worship to Monday Work* (Crossway, 2011).

William Pollard, *The Soul of the Firm* (HarperCollins, 1996).

Larry Peabody, *Secular Work is Full-time Service.* (Christian Literature Crusade, 1974).

Shirley Roels, "The Christian Calling To Business," *Theology Today* 60 (2003): 357-69.

Amy Sherman, *Kingdom Calling: Vocational Stewardship for the Common Good* (InterVarsity Press, 2012).

Doug Sherman and William Hendricks, *Your Work Matters to God* (Navigator Press, 1987).

Max Stackhouse, Dennis McCann and Shirley Roels, eds., *On Moral Business* (Eerdmans, 1995).

Other resources can be found at:

http://www.spu.edu/holycalling (website for *Business as a Holy Calling?*)

http://spu.libguides.com/workandfaith (Seattle Pacific University has an excellent collection of resources on work and faith)

http://www.businessasmission.com (Business as Mission Global Think Tank)

http://www.spu.edu/academics/center-for-integrity-in-business (Seattle Pacific University)

http://oikonomianetwork.org (Network of seminaries, professors committed to integrating work and faith)

http://www.madetoflourish.org (Network of pastors wanting to equip and support Christians in their daily work life)

http://www.economicwisdom.org

http://www.faithandwork.com (Redeemer Church, NYC)

http://depree.org (Fuller Theological Seminary)

http://marketplace.regent-college.edu (Regent College)

http://www.centerforfaithandbusiness.com (Concordia University)

http://www.licc.org.uk/resources/resources-2/work-forum/ (London Institute for Contemporary Christianity Work Forum)

http://www.transformingbusiness.net/ (Cambridge University)

http://www.povertycure.org/issues/enterprise-solutions-to-poverty/

http://www.centerforfinancialinclusion.org

http://www.c3leaders.com/just-business-roundtable. (Network of Christian business persons committed to serving in business by living in community, engaging in commerce, and impacting culture)

http://www.bcorporation.net (standards for triple bottom line "B Corporations")

www.faithandleadership.com (Duke University)

http://www.princeton.edu/faithandwork/ (Faith and work initiative of Princeton University)

http://eventidefunds.com/faith-and-business/ (articles on aspects of faith and business)

ACKNOWLEDGEMENTS

I begin by giving thanks to my wife Kerry. For over 40 years we've journeyed together and she's graced my life with her support, wisdom, encouragement, and deep love. In regard to this book itself, its content is greatly enriched by her profound theological insights, relational wisdom, and clarity of thought.

This project has been a long-term group effort. Over the decades, Barry Rowan, Jeff Van Duzer, Rodger Voorhies, and Bruce Baker have guided me in my understanding of business as a Christian vocation. They've helped bring realism as well as faith into my perspective. For a year, Bruce Kennedy (former President of Alaska Airlines) and I met with a group of Christian CEOs to explore these ideas. Colleagues who have been faculty of Regent College in Vancouver have given me insight and inspiration, especially Paul Stevens and Walt Wright. Students at Regent College and in Seattle Pacific University's MBA program helped shape the content.

I'm grateful for Scott Brown and the 5,000 staff of World Vision International's Vision Fund, which provides micro-loans to millions of families around the world. They have engaged in depth with the ideas in this book to explore their pertinence in struggling economies for people emerging from poverty.

More recently, faculty colleagues at the Seattle Pacific University School of Business, Government, and Economics; School of Theology and Seattle Pacific Seminary; Center for Integrity in Business; and Center for Biblical and Theological Education have provided key insights. Through a grant from the Kern Family Foundation, many small groups of seminary students, church, and business leaders have worked through drafts of this material in detail. I'm especially grateful to Celeste Cranston and Eli Ritchie at SPU's Center for Biblical and Theological Education.

About the Author

For over 35-years Tim Dearborn has worked with people in a range of professions and occupations, to help them find the connection between their work and the purposes of God. He has served as a professor for Regent College in Vancouver, BC, and in the School of Business and Economics at Seattle Pacific University. For ten years he worked in the executive office of World Vision International. He has a PhD in Theology and Masters degrees in comparative religion and cross-cultural communication.

He currently serves as the Director of the Lloyd John Ogilvie Institute of Preaching at Fuller Theological Seminary, as well as leads the program of "Business Integration Groups" through Seattle Pacific University's Schools of Theology and Business and Economics. He lives in Seattle with his wife, Kerry, who is a Professor of Theology at Seattle Pacific University. Three grown daughters, their husbands, and six grandchildren enrich their lives.

He is the author or editor of 15 books or monographs on mission, spirituality and leadership related topics.
Relevant to *Business as a Holy Calling?* are:

Making Life Right: Reflections on Micah 6:8 (2016)
Beyond Duty: A Passion for Christ, a Heart for Mission (2013)
Grace-Shaped Leadership (2011)
Reflections on Business and Micro-Enterprise Development (2009)
Reflections on Marketing and Fundraising (2009)
Reflections on Advocacy and Justice (2009)
Biblical Wisdom for Financial Crises (2008)

For information about these or other resources, or to contact the author see: www.dynamisresources.com

Made in the USA
Lexington, KY
30 September 2019